Ailsa Fabian was born in Melbourne, where her mother, with two sisters, built up a thriving fashion business in the years after World War One. Ailsa assumed that, like them, work outside the home would always be central to her life. She lectured in history at Melbourne University before studying sociology at Columbia University, New York, and, after moving to London in 1952, worked in social research and in the fashion business. Then, following marriage to the sculptor Erwin Fabian and the birth of her daughter, she became so entranced by the miracle of Sarah's unfolding engagement with the world, that she chose to be an-almost-full-time mother.

When Sarah died in 1964 while on a family visit to Australia, Ailsa turned to writing. She had published various sociological studies, but *The Daniel Diary*, which records the reactions of her three-year-old son to his sister's death, was her first literary work. It is now followed by *The Sarah Journals*.

Ailsa Fabian lives in London and Majorca.

AILSA FABIAN

The Sarah *Journals*

Surviving Tragedy without God

Copyright © 2011 Ailsa Fabian

The moral right of the author has been asserted.

Apart from any fair dealing for the purposes of research or private study, or criticism or review, as permitted under the Copyright, Designs and Patents Act 1988, this publication may only be reproduced, stored or transmitted, in any form or by any means, with the prior permission in writing of the publishers, or in the case of reprographic reproduction in accordance with the terms of licences issued by the Copyright Licensing Agency. Enquiries concerning reproduction outside those terms should be sent to the publishers.

Matador
5 Weir Road
Kibworth Beauchamp
Leicester LE8 0LQ, UK
Tel: (+44) 116 279 2299
Fax: (+44) 116 279 2277
Email: books@troubador.co.uk
Web: www.troubador.co.uk/matador

ISBN SB: 978 1848766 341
HB: 9781848766365

British Library Cataloguing in Publication Data.
A catalogue record for this book is available from the British Library.

Typeset in 12pt Adone Garamond Pro by Troubador Publishing Ltd, Leicester, UK
Printed and bound in the UK by TJI Digital, Padstow, Cornwall

Matador is an imprint of Troubador Publishing Ltd

MIX
Paper from
responsible sources
FSC
www.fsc.org
FSC® C013056

*In memory of Naomi Lewis,
poet, critic, teacher, friend.*

'It takes a very long time to understand lived experience.'
Stuart Hampshire

'Montaigne, to recover from the death of La Boétie, needed to write the *Essais*, no less.'
André Comte-Sponville

'What interests me are the immediate reactions to daily events, the ideas which come and would otherwise so quickly go, the unexpected and often unsuitable emotions. In other words, I now find the current of any life far more absorbing than the large remembered 'events'; the reconstructed pattern.'
Philip Toynbee

CONTENTS

I An Ending, 1964	1
II First Questions, 1964-1965	20
III A Diary of Grief, 1965-1966	40
IV A Homecoming, 1966-1970	52
V New Ventures, 1970-1983	78
VI Something Done, 1983-1988	116
VII Getting Published, 1988-1992	133
VIII New Texts, 1993-1994	175
IX Afterwords, 2000 - Infinity	203
Summary of Contents	239
Acknowledgments	244

I

An Ending
1964

In the early dark of a winter evening, I carried her down the drive to the waiting ambulance. Erwin and her small brother Daniel stood on the pavement, waving goodbye as we drove off. It was our last moment together as a happy optimistic family.

The weekend had begun unremarkably. On Saturday we had gone to the market, called on a friend to admire her new flat, and visited an exhibition of Indian handcrafts, where I bought Sarah a red linen bag embroidered with silks and little mirrors, vivid, like her. On Sunday morning the children played cheerfully in the garden. But late in the afternoon she seemed tired and grumpy and I put her to bed early in my room. She didn't protest, although before that she had been asking impatiently if it was time for a favourite television programme.

In the night she woke with croup and we called a doctor, who gave her a penicillin injection. Next morning she had a high temperature and her breathing was intermittently laboured and croupy. At those moments she was plainly in distress, but in between she became again her ebullient five-year-old self, laughing and joking with

Daniel. Erwin and I sat with her in turn, and I read her favourite stories. She was visited by two of the doctors from the group practice. In the evening we called in a consultant paediatrician, who said she should go to hospital. 'Will you stay with me until I settle down?' she asked. I put a toothbrush in my bag, in case I could stay with her overnight.

At the Royal Melbourne Children's Hospital we were shown into a bright little room stocked with toys and children's books. The young doctor who listened to her breathing said, 'You were right to bring her in, but she'll be alright.' A wheelchair was produced. 'I want to sit on your knee,' she said. We were taken up to a glass-walled lobby, with the city spread out below like a vast shining sea. 'Look – the lights of the city,' I said, but she was too languid to respond. Suddenly her chair was pivoted around and she vanished. I moved to follow her, but a nurse pushed me into a small waiting-room, with the remark that 'You can see her when we have put her to bed.'

I waited a long time, patiently reading the book I had brought with me. The building was silent; it might have been completely deserted. Finally two doctors appeared and questioned me. What colour had she been when I last saw her? Had she been blue? No, her face had been flushed. They went away but quickly returned, and told me that she had died. I accepted the truth of what they said at once, with stupefied comprehension. Erwin was summoned by telephone and together we went to see her. She lay in bed looking as if asleep, beautiful, herself. 'Can't you do something?' I asked the doctor. He shook his head.

AN ENDING

We left the hospital in which she lay dead, to begin life without her. It seemed impossible to go calmly home, and we walked in a nearby park, under a row of harsh yellow lights, in cold misty air. I was dazed, understanding the direness and irrevocability of what had happened, but as if from an immense distance, without any turmoil of passion or protest.

In the yellow misty light, under the leafless trees, little more than an hour after her death, I made the first big decision of my new life. With the cool lucidity of shock, I reflected that although her marvellous gifts of love and energy were now useless to her, and her joyful intensity of living and discovering had vanished, the miracle of her being must not be wasted. I would preserve and share it by writing about her, a spurt of exaltation that was the prelude to a long period of stunned misery.

Life implacably continued. That first morning, after a sleepless night, I got up to make tea for my father, and to telephone a friend to say I would not be ferrying the children to nursery school that morning. Erwin and I continued to do what was needed to keep daily existence going in a household that included Daniel, Erwin's mother and my father. But only two activities really engaged us – sharing our grief with each other, and arranging her funeral. We had loved her equally and had been equally blessed by her unbounded love. We knew that we felt the same sense of utter devastation, and we could acknowledge and find brief comfort in sharing that awareness through a look, a gesture or a few words. If in later years we have seldom talked at any length about how her death has affected our inner being, the knowledge that his continued love and longing for her is as profound as my own has been a source of strength.

The day after she died, we took Mama and Daniel to see her as she lay in bed in a small room near the hospital chapel, with the hospital's tribute of a plastic rose on the pillow. I placed beside her the little primer *Horse* which I had recently given her; we would have read it together in the reading lessons which had been an intense and hopeful sharing. But I was acutely aware that she was no longer present. What lay on the bed was simply a corpse. I did not stay long.

Instead, I went to see the Medical Director of the Children's Hospital. He was generous with his time and we had several long talks with him. He had not been on duty that night but had rushed into the hospital on being informed that a patient had died. It was almost unheard of these days for a five-year-old to die of a respiratory infection, he said, but she had stopped breathing soon after she arrived in the ward, and an attempted tracheotomy had failed. I grilled Dr G on the implications of each detail of events in the hospital. 'It's easier for the mothers of most of the children we see here,' he remarked. 'They have more faith.' 'In divine providence?' I asked. 'No,' he said, 'in the medical profession.'

He talked to us without any defensive parade of authority, as to equals. But the inequality remained. We had been savagely wounded and he was unscathed, a contrast grotesquely underlined the last time I saw him by the coincidence that his wife had just given birth to their first child. He strode round the room, grinning triumphantly and tossing a pencil into the air, as he answered our woeful questions.

There had to be a funeral. Neither Erwin nor I was a follower of any established religion. I had retained from the Protestant services and sermons of my boarding-school days only a mild contempt. I don't know that Erwin had ever been to synagogue in his life, but he understood the Jewish attitude to death to be one of uncompromising severity, which he respected. We went to see a liberal rabbi who persuaded us, gently and sympathetically, that Sarah was Jewish neither by birth nor by upbringing, and a Jewish service would not be fitting. So we drew up our own order of service. We visited various 'Funeral Parlours', looking for one that was not too repulsive, drove half-way to Geelong to inspect a new crematorium, and ordered a sheath of early spring flowers. I made a pale-blue velvet pall to cover her coffin. All this filled up time, and gave us the illusion that we were still doing something for her.

On the morning of the funeral, we looked at her body for the last time. She lay in her coffin, looking even less like herself than on the previous occasion. The wooden box gripped her tightly, a vivid demonstration of the grave's narrowness. We cut a lock of her hair as a keepsake, and I stuffed into the coffin her piggy-pillow. 'We forgot piggy,' she had said when we had arrived at the hospital a week earlier, and I had promised to bring him to her. Erwin added the necklace of crystal beads which he had given her for her birthday. We joined a group of invited friends waiting in the hospital courtyard, and a small procession drove through the industrial suburbs towards the crematorium.

We had asked Douglas Gasking, Professor of Philosophy at Melbourne University, to conduct the service and read the lesson. Two Melbourne philosophers, George Paul and Dan Taylor, had had an immense influence on me as a student, and on many of my generation, but George was in Oxford and Dan in New Zealand. Douglas was their friend and fellow-spirit, a tall fair-haired man with a solid presence and a sonorous voice, who read with authority the passages from Ecclesiastes we had chosen.

> ... Whatsoever thy hand findeth to do, do it with thy might; for there is no work nor device nor knowledge nor wisdom in the grave whither thou goest.

> ... For man also knoweth not his time: as the fishes that are taken in an evil net, and as the birds that are caught in the snare; so are the sons of men snared in an evil time, when it falleth suddenly upon them... All go unto one place; all are of the dust, and all turn to dust again. Who knoweth the spirit of man that goeth upward, and the spirit of the beast that goeth downward to the earth? ...

Bleak words certainly. Consolatory? I don't know. I thought they stated the truth, and that anything less would have been unworthy of her.

AN ENDING

Nan Hutton spoke about Sarah, and her words were gentler. They are the only description of her I possess that I have not written myself, and when I reread them many years later, they brought her vividly close.

> Sarah was the daughter of my friends and the friend of my children. And she was also my friend. This was because Sarah didn't have to stay with her own age group, she could choose a friend anywhere. And now that we have to say goodbye to her, this is one of her qualities that seems unforgettable – Sarah's wonderful gift for friendship that sprang from a very loving heart and a quick and curious mind.
>
> She was lovely to look at and she had most endearing ways. She was also one of the rare children who are not only perceptive, but able to communicate thoughts and feelings without hesitation and without inhibition.
>
> In fact Sarah felt everything so intensely that she seemed *forced* to communicate. She told me almost nothing at all without hopping up and down in the excitement of the moment. She brought this intensity to everything she did. Her life was short, but she lived every moment of it fully. She was happy, she was rich in love, she brought delight.
>
> We cannot evade now our own anguish since we have lost Sarah. But I am sure we should not feel anguish for her, only for ourselves because we

cannot help that. She knew so many joys, and she knew how to be grateful.

I should like to read you now the child's poem through which she expressed her thanksgiving. Sarah learned this at kindergarten and she tried to teach it to Dan, but she always got it wrong in one line. And then she would often think of a great many more things to give thanks for, so the thanksgiving would sometimes go on for a long time. Here we have one of Sarah's own versions.

Thank you for the food we eat,
Thank you for the world so sweet,
Thank you God for everything,
Thank you everyone that sings.
Thank you for the rabbits
Thank you for the fishes
Thank you for the possums
Thank you for the flowers.

And I think we should now say 'Thank you for Sarah.'

I remember the funeral now with astonishment that we could have deliberately planned and calmly sat through it, at a time when we were overwhelmed by the unreal and devastating knowledge of her eternal absence. But the need to act with respect and ceremony towards the remains of the dead is as strong among unbelievers as among the followers of every religion there has ever been. She who has been the centre of our love and attention no longer exists, but we cannot suddenly withdraw that love and care. We continue to behave towards her, as much as is in our power, as if she still exists. The loving attention will become increasingly private, inward, hidden. The funeral is the last time she will play a central role in a social gathering. With the help of Douglas and Nan, we had done the best we could, and I felt that the occasion was worthy of her.

I lived through the following weeks in a state of what I can only call emotional pain, a state that, like physical pain, absorbs one's entire attention and drains the sense of reality from everything else. I could scarcely think of anything but the ineluctable and yet totally unacceptable fact of her death. I went through the days in a frozen awareness of the emptiness where she should have been. In the evening, a stiff drink before dinner and then a sleeping tablet softened the edges of reality and brought a measure of relief, but at four o'clock each morning the knowledge that she was dead pierced my sleep like a searchlight. Weeks passed before a day I remember clearly, when for the first time, waking to the same anguished truth, I thought 'It won't go away, it can wait', and sank back into sleep.

I could look after Daniel, run the household, and prepare meals but, if I had to go into town, I reacted to its energy and super-abundant materialism with revulsion. Standing on the escalator at Myers, where I had gone to buy pyjamas for Daniel, I looked down at the crowds and the close-packed displays in utter panic.

The first social occasion I ventured to attend promised to be innocuous enough – a lecture in a friend's house in aid of some charity, followed by coffee. I followed the speaker's words, more or less, but afterwards, holding a coffee cup and facing an acquaintance, I was unable to utter even a banal comment. I slipped out quietly and went home.

Erwin and I struggled to understand how, without any warning, she could suddenly vanish from the world. We both believed, at least some of the time, that Sarah should not have died – that some small addition of concern or observation, an earlier or a different decision, would have saved her. There had been hesitations, blurrings, confusions, small carelessnesses, delays and reversals of treatment, and it was easy to speculate, reasonably and convincingly, that if at this or that moment someone had acted differently, she would still be alive.

We asked the hospital for a report, which they agreed to give us only when we told them we wanted to send it to our brother-in-law Dr André Cournand, eminent physician and Nobel laureate. In technical language, the report described the onset of her illness, the admission to hospital, her collapse after arriving in the ward, the attempts to revive her and an unsuccessful tracheotomy. Despite the suddenness of the crisis, she did not lack immediate medical attention. The resident doctor for the ward was present, and the medical registrar arrived soon after. The report concluded:

Postmortem examination revealed an extensive

laryngo-tracheobronchitis with thick yellow-green mucopus obstructing the minor and major bronchi. There was not a great deal of parenchymatous involvement. Influenza virus, strain A2, was isolated from a bronchial swab. No positive bacterial culture was obtained but the presence of thick mucopus in the bronchi clearly indicated bacterial superinfection and this was presumably staphylococcal in nature.

This told us, impersonally and in a little more detail, what we already knew, but it didn't seem enough. Erwin asked me to write a more detailed account of her illness and, painfully and reluctantly, I described the events of her last day, her behaviour and ours, the visits of the various doctors and their comments and recommendations, the journey to hospital, and as much as I knew of what happened there.

We sent copies of the two reports to medical friends in Australia, New York and London. Of course, uselessly. The Melbourne professor said nothing. André Cournand wrote with sympathy but unjudgmentally. Dr Adler, the physician who had delivered her and whom we loved and respected as a friend, remarked flatly, in London, later, that she had clearly been 'misdiagnosed'. Only George Shaw, an old friend now in general practice, made any helpful comment. He acknowledged that there were many moments which could have changed the outcome, but pointed out that for some of them the alternative could well have seemed at the time more fraught with danger, and that children's volatility even in sickness makes every decision difficult. I put the reports away and have not looked at them again, except, reluctantly, to write this summary.

For Daniel, who was not yet three, her death must have been even more devastating than it was for Erwin and me. She had burst relatively late into our adult lives, in an explosion of love and wonder, but Daniel had never known life without her; the two children had not been separated for a single day. She was the elder sister, sometimes bossy, more often tenderly protective; he was her devoted slave and court jester. 'I always make Sarah laugh,' he said once after she died, with precocious self-understanding. They played together, rarely fought, and confronted the treacheries of the adult world, on the rare occasions, for example, when we went out to dinner, as staunch allies.

With her death, Daniel's demeanour changed radically. Laughter vanished and he rarely smiled; he became solemn and subdued. And while Erwin and I were bewildered by the suddenness of her disappearance, I knew that his incomprehension must be much deeper. I attempted to explain her death to him in plain words, and we took him to see her dead body in the hospital, though not to the funeral. Over the months that followed, I often talked to him of Sarah, of how much he missed her, and our own sadness, and how helpless we and the doctors had been to save her. I tried to answer his questions, especially about where she had gone, in ways he might understand, without

AN ENDING

transgressing my own beliefs more than seemed unavoidable. Often, in the end, I accepted his own imaginative answers. I kept a record of our conversations, which was published many years later as *The Daniel Diary*. Gradually his memories of her faded until we rarely mentioned her. But his whole life has been marked by her death.

I have not written more about Daniel's grief, or his continuing life, in these diaries, out of respect for his privacy, and because I am essentially recording my own experience. Yet Daniel's existence, my love for him, the work of looking after him, watching him grow and sharing his life was a positive, essential and blessed part of my own life during the period covered by these diaries, and beyond. Joy and woe are woven fine. I can scarcely imagine the desolation of parents without children, those parents whose only child has died, or who have lost all their children.

I continued for a long time to pore over the events of her last day, weighing up the behaviour of doctors and nurses and the ambulance driver and myself, examining the moments at which it was possible to think that she could have been saved. I didn't share these cross-examinations with Erwin, and never considered, even privately, how he might have behaved differently. Nor has he ever expressed the slightest criticism of my actions. He may have made his own self-accusations. Years later he said to me, 'You know what cannot be said.' I inferred that he was speaking of the day of Sarah's death.

My worst anguish, then and for many years, concerned

the memory of that moment in the glass-walled hospital lobby when I was brusquely and finally parted from her. I had promised her that I would stay with her until she 'settled down' and then I had let her be whisked away from me, and meekly allowed myself to be pushed into a waiting-room. A failure and a betrayal. 'Was she crying?' I asked Dr G. 'Yes.' 'And if she had not cried, she might have been able to continue breathing?' 'Possibly.' If I had stayed with her, she would not have cried. And the nurses? It was not hospital policy to separate parent and child like that, Dr G said, but they had told him that there had been 'chaos in the ward' – i.e. several children had been crying perhaps, or refusing to stay in bed. It is almost unbearable to reflect that her life might have hung on those few instants.

And universally discouraged. Even Freud calls such inevitable speculations 'entirely unfounded self-reproaches.' And if, ten minutes later, I had been called to her bedside and had found her happy to see me and breathing normally, I would not have accused myself of anything. I acknowledge (without conviction) the argument that 'You're not a doctor; if the doctors did not see that there was an acute crisis, how could you have?' And she might have died even if I had stayed with her. An argument or perhaps a scuffle with the nurses wouldn't have helped. At times I have thought I could gladly murder those nurses, but they didn't know she was about to die, either.

What happened happened, and in the end there is no point in continuing to imagine that it might have been otherwise. But I don't agree that self-reproaches are always without foundation or useless. Sometimes they are clearly baseless, like those of the mother who sent her ten-year-old son on an errand to the corner shop, in the course of which he was set upon and battered to death by a teenage gang. But others of us might have been, should have been, wiser or quicker to understand, or more loyal. For myself, it was necessary to look minutely again and again at every one of those possible turning-points, before I could come near to accepting her death as unalterable fact. I have to remind myself that she died because of the pullulation of bacteria within her body. Of 'natural causes'. But I also see human imperfection woven into the tangle of cause and effect that brought about her death, as into everything we do. Most of the time, with sorrow and pity, I manage, more or less, to forgive the doctors, the nurses, and myself.

I never wept for her, then or later. I associated tears with wilfulness and self-dramatisation – in scenes with early lovers, when I argued and contradicted and refused invitations and then felt abandoned and worked myself into paroxysms of weeping; and after one real betrayal, when I cried uncontrollably for days; and in outbreaks of self-pity and rage at Erwin when the children were small and I felt overburdened and thought he didn't do his share. All those tears for myself! They would be a despicable indulgence after such a final tragedy.

For weeks I used to go eagerly down to the gate after breakfast to collect the mail, hoping there would be letters about her. 'Longing for mail is longing to hear that Sarah is not dead,' I noted. And I wanted to break the silence that had engulfed her; I wanted her to still exist in the shared social world. Most of the letters were conventional, with scarcely a phrase worth remembering among the lot. Yet I welcomed them all, and never turned my anger and resentment on even the most inarticulate writer, as I did when someone spoke words that jarred (as almost anything was liable to). And I seethed with fury against some of those who did not write, who didn't exonerate themselves from suspicion of collusion in her death. I resented especially two who later told me they had not written 'on principle'. I never asked what principle, but it took me years to forgive them.

I was astonished at the way society tacitly accepted her death. No enquiry, no inquest, no doctor called in to give a second opinion, no policeman knocking at the door, no protest in the papers, no outcry anywhere! And the death of a child, unlike that of a husband or wife, doesn't entail a multitude of duties and decisions. There is more spare time – back to caring for one child instead of two – but once the funeral is over, not much that has to be done. I collected her death certificate from a cavernous basement office. Someone must have registered her death, the only official act demanded. It was neither Erwin nor me.

Not many private duties either, and no pressure to perform them. Two years later I gave away most of her clothes, but kept some of her favourite dresses, which I packed away in a suitcase with her favourite stuffed toys. Eventually I applied for probate on her modest estate, and succeeded in redeeming and transferring to Daniel the National Savings Certificates my mother had given her. But I never did manage to assemble the documents needed to cash her premium bond, though the clerks in Newcastle were patient and sympathetic. I disposed of a few more of her possessions over the years. Some I still keep.

After the funeral was over and the brief words of condolence uttered, no-one mentioned her name. She might never have existed. The silence was a chilling surprise. Erwin and I thought of her all the time, and talked of her often, but when we were with other people, there was only a desolate emptiness where she had been. 'But what on earth could we say?' I would have been glad of any scrap of recollection or murmur of regret. When we visited friends in the country, I longed for them to say, 'What a pity Sarah isn't here. She would have loved to see the calves.' Even now, when news of children is exchanged, I sometimes think that those who know she once existed should ask, 'And how is Sarah?'

Oswald Burt, the chairman of our family company in Melbourne, often spoke of his only son, who had been killed in the war. After Sarah died, I understood that he must have decided that if his son were to remain in the world, he himself would have to keep him there. I came to admire his courage and persistence. My attempts to talk about Sarah were less successful. If I mentioned her in a normal tone of voice, I was liable to be silenced by a murmured commonplace and a pantomine of sympathy for something too painful to speak of. Occasionally I could break through this repressive embarrassment, but mostly I let myself be censored.

I read out to Erwin a passage from the sociologist Erving Goffman about 'cooling the mark'. When a gang of racecourse conmen has brought off a successful scam and is making off with the spoils, one of them stays behind to persuade the victim to accept his loss and not call the police – to cool the mark. 'That's us,' Erwin said. Yes, all three of us, victims whose protests had been muffled by doctors, priests, rabbis, the Registrar of Deaths, funeral directors, newspaper proprietors, acquaintances, strangers, family and friends. By the whole weight of society which didn't care about understanding or justice or redemption but only about avoiding discomfort. For them all, and for reality itself, we were marks to be cooled. OK, we shut up, but with a sense of isolation and resentment.

Cecily de Monchaux, university lecturer in psychology, psychoanalyst and a close friend, came to stay with us. She had known and loved Sarah since birth, and Sarah had loved her. She had also, I think, observed us all professionally, as case-study material. Telling me about her case-consultations with Donald Winnicott, whom she admired profoundly, she said, 'He knows about Sarah.' And so he should, I thought. A miraculous being who had grown and flourished without the help of his profession.

Cecily was the only person with whom we were able to talk easily and naturally about Sarah's death and our own devastation. We talked for many hours. It brought relief to share even the most obvious comment ('There's absolutely nothing you can do'). She kept me company while I cleared from beside Sarah's bed her treasured possessions: a purple silk ribbon, several postcards of animals, a leaflet about the platypus (a 'map', she had called it), a few foreign coins and the last book we had read together.

AN ENDING

When we had telephoned Cecily in London to tell her of Sarah's death, her immediate response had been positive. 'How wonderful that she was,' she said through her tears. In the years to come, I often thought of that tribute as I struggled to overcome the sorrow, protest, bewilderment and despair which frequently overshadowed gratitude for her life.

II

First Questions
1964-1965

'You need strong beliefs to survive something like this,' Cecily said. I welcomed this traditionally humane comment when she might have trotted out psychoanalytical clichés. She could be as dismissive of non-analytical explanations as any of her colleagues. 'Autobiography always seems to me just uninterpreted material,' she once told me, when I was already an addicted reader, though not yet a writer, of autobiography.

There is little mention of beliefs in current professional writing about mourning, only an occasional perfunctory acknowledgment that faith in God and confidence in the life hereafter can be a support. Cecily was not thinking of these, which she knew I did not share. What takes their place for the non-believer? Did I have strong beliefs and did they help me survive? Or did I survive through those I acquired after she died? Not questions it is possible to answer simply. They are, I suppose, the subject of this book.

The beliefs I had when she died (the relevant ones) were those basic non-beliefs – no God and no after-life; she had utterly ceased to exist; her early death was the consequence of a tangle of chance happenings. Negative beliefs, but I held them strongly. And I think they did help me survive. By their unchallengeability. By a certain pride in not wavering. But in a sheltered previous existence I had never needed the support of strong beliefs, and these were skeletal and untested. I have spent decades contemplating, repeating, clarifying and enlarging them; in reading widely and building up a personal anthology of pronouncements and instances and the experiences of others; in thinking about Sarah's life and her death, about life and death and mourning and consolation and the nature of the universe; in coming to know what I already knew.

At first I focussed on the desperate longing to find something, anything, to set against the destruction and waste of her death and mitigate the terrible sense of desolation. Profound grief was new to me; I had no beliefs about it. I tried to recall books that might help, but a bookish past had left me with little of any use. I searched in vain for a half-remembered Dostoyevsky saying that 'sorrow is a teacher'. About all I salvaged from past reading were a few lines from Blake.

> Joy and woe are woven fine,
> A clothing for the soul divine;
> Under every grief and pine
> Runs a joy with silken twine.
> It is right it should be so;
> Man was made for joy and woe;
> And when this we rightly know,
> Thro' the world we safely go.

This must have seemed at first more a promise than a truth, but it was hopeful, and I repeated it to myself, then and in the years to come and still now. In those early weeks I also concocted arguments of my own that seemed to offer a measure of consolation.

The death of a child is an unbearable outrage. But could the world have been so constituted that no child would die, and death only begin to strike after some minimum qualifying age? Clearly a ridiculous notion. Imagine the paralysing terror as the ominous year approached. Since all must die (I never doubted that), death at any age, even of the very young, must be accepted.

Then, I had wanted her to experience life to the full. But unpredictable chance, including that of death at any moment, is an inextricable part of life. So she had indeed experienced the life I wanted for her and which I longed to give her. A curious argument whose logic I don't understand, but it did at the time seem to offer the support of incontrovertible truth.

And a discovery that has been made countless times, one of the true and enduring consolations: if I had not loved her so deeply I would not suffer so much; pain was the price I must pay for the love and happiness which I could not wish to have forgone, and for having shared a life that I could not wish unlived.

'Time is the only thing that can help,' people said. I longed for the peace of that time when enough time should have passed. Six months to a year was apparently thought sufficient. It didn't seem nearly long enough and I didn't want it to be. Then Barbara Falk, who had befriended us out of sympathy, said: 'It takes eight years,' and I felt gratefully reassured.

New habits helped. Singing to myself, silently or aloud, a song from an old Nelson Eddy film:

Keep right on to the end of the road,
Keep right on to the end...

I relished the words, the tune, the thumping rhythm, and the image of Nelson Eddy, with his rosy skin and toothpaste smile, on horseback, pretending to be a Canadian Mountie, and singing as he rode. I told myself to keep right on, and knew that I must, but I also rejected with contempt the possibility of keeping on without her. I sang both to encourage and to ridicule myself, to deflect attention from reality onto words, and because singing was in itself a pleasure that fleetingly tempered pain. (Only many years later did I learn that this was written by Harry Lauder and widely known, far beyond the context of a Nelson Eddy film.)

I started to collect instances of persons whose grief lasted a long while: the wife of philosopher John Dewey who 'never recovered' from the death of a child; Dame Enid Lyons, the doughty widow of Australian Prime Minister Joe Lyons, who had borne twelve children one of whom died in infancy, and who said, 'Every time I hear someone mention my eleven children, I think silently, no, twelve'; Leonard Woolf's brother Philip, who had seen a third brother, Cecil, killed at his side in France during the 1914 war, and who also 'never completely recovered.' Many years later, at the end of a hard-working and successful life, after his wife died, Philip committed suicide – because, I inferred from Leonard's account, he no longer saw any reason to struggle against grief for his brother.

I did not talk about all this arguing and searching, not even to Erwin. He felt no need to reiterate the obvious, perhaps because he had encountered tragedy at a much earlier age, having left his home and homeland under the threat of Nazi persecution, as had other members of his Berlin Jewish family; those who remained behind had been murdered. 'I know when something is over,' he said when I spoke of persistent and disconcerting spurts of hope that she might return. For him, the only thing to do was to get on with his own work as painter and sculptor. So I did not discuss my theorising with him, or with anyone else.

Instead, I turned to writing. With a nanny to look after Daniel on weekdays, I retired with my typewriter to a glassed-in upstairs balcony overlooking treetops and the gabled roofs of Victorian outhouses. All sorts of writing, for the most part private and intended to remain so, writing in the sense of putting words on paper, not in the sense of creating a considered and shareable text. I held long sessions of repetitive, undisciplined monologue in which I looked at the events of her death over and over again, commented on my own reactions, recalled the past, and poured out my love and longing for Sarah and my outrage at her fate. I have kept the entire accumulation of these densely-covered pages of free-association stashed away in brown envelopes, but I seldom look at them. If occasionally now I open one of the envelopes and reread a page or two, I return painfully to the atmosphere of those early months, but the language is too diffuse and banal to be quoted, and the record boring to read at length, even for me. I can no more offer a sample of it than I could provide a sample of a long-past bout of weeping. But these unshareable outpourings were my true and spontaneous lament for her.

In a different mood, I started to work on the book about Sarah which I hoped might eventually be published, by noting down everything I could remember about her – impressions, incidents, fragments of talk, favourite words, anything however trivial, recorded in sessions at the typewriter, in notebooks I carried round with me, and on odd scraps of paper. Rereading these early notes years later, I was surprised at how clear, perceptive, and elegantly expressed many of them are, though written in numbing misery, but it was a long time before I managed to transform them into a respectable-seeming text. Once, about a year after she died, I started to write a continuous narrative, but when I came to tell of her birth in hospital, I remembered that other hospital in which her life had ended, and was paralysed by despair. The effort was premature for another reason – I hadn't learned enough about writing. I may have been able to shape a few good sentences, but I didn't know how to put them together, or what to include and what to leave out. It took long study of other people's books (the beginning writer reads in an entirely new way), and practice on less momentous subjects, before I achieved a first draft.

About a year after Sarah's death, Barbara Falk asked

what I was doing, and I told her that I was working on a book about Sarah. She did not approve. 'You can't live your life in mourning,' she said, and 'I can see that it might do you some good, but I can't see that it will be any use to anyone else.' I looked at what I was doing in the light of these judgments, wanting to prove them wrong, but the resolution to write about her was unshaken. To produce a book that captured her intensity, her joyous exuberance and astonishing inventiveness, a book that would be worthy of her and do her honour, became a central and sustaining purpose of my life.

Writing was intertwined with reading. When I had two children, and a demanding involvement in a family business, I had no time to visit libraries and I read less than at any other time in my life. After Sarah's death, a friend made a practical gesture of sympathy by offering me a spare set of tickets for the neighbouring Camberwell library, which had a new airy building and an up-to-date stock, in contrast to our grimy run-down local library. As a graduate of Melbourne University, I was entitled to borrow books from its libraries. Camberwell offered new publications, and chance discoveries, the University enabled me to track down classic texts. I read about death and grief and mourning, about children, about writing and diaries and memory, copying extracts and writing comments on them. The deluge of published discussion, and in particular of personal testimonies, about death and mourning and childbirth and new parenthood which burst upon us in the last decades of the twentieth century was still to come; I found few books on any of these subjects; but in a haphazard way I did come across texts that spoke strongly and pertinently to me. Too many to list, or even remember, but these are some from which I learned.

On the Camberwell shelves I came across James Agee's novel *A Death in the Family*. A father to his suddenly-widowed daughter:.

> You've got to bear it in mind that nobody that ever lived is specially privileged; the axe can fall at any moment, on any neck, without any warning or any regard for justice. You've got to keep your mind off pitying your own rotten luck and setting up any kind of a howl about it…

'Yes, I agree', I noted, though Erwin, when I showed him the passage, merely said impatiently, 'Of course.' Now I squirm at this patronising sanctimoniousness. I'm thankful no-one talked to me like that. But such statements were new to me and I welcomed them. The father continues:

> It's a kind of test, Mary, and it's the only kind that amounts to anything. When something rotten like this happens. Then you have your choice. You start to really be alive, or you start to die. That's all.

'Not for us,' I wrote. 'What made us start to live was the glimpse of paradise with Sarah and Daniel. Her death is blighting and destroying not only for Sarah but for us. If we somehow manage to stay alive, it will be in spite of it, in no sense because of it. It is true that I had no experience of death before, but I had no experience of family love either, and that was the life-giving thing.'

I had heard of only one book by a bereaved parent, *Death be not Proud*, by John Gunther, whose son Johnny died of a brain tumour at the age of seventeen. I looked for a copy, and tracked it down to the Melbourne University Medical School Library. Notice of my arrival had to be telephoned ahead, and I was met by the librarian wearing a white coat. She happened to be someone I had known when we were both students, and I felt shamefully exposed, an illegitimate intruder into medical mysteries. The notes that I made at the time are severe. I wanted to find companionship in grief and I did, but already, two months after she died, I was also looking for hints on how to write about a dead child, and how not to, and I found John Gunther often wanting.

In Ernest Jones's Life of Freud, I learned of Ernst Brücke, the eminent nineteenth-century physiologist who was one of Freud's teachers.

> A Protestant, with his Prussian speech, he must have seemed out of place in easy-going Catholic Vienna, an emissary from another and more austere world – as indeed he was... The general opinion had him labelled as a cold, purely rational man. What degree of violent force against himself and his emotions he needed to build up this front is revealed by his reaction to the death of his beloved son in 1873. He forbade his family and friends to

mention his son's name, put all pictures of him out of sight, and worked even harder than before.

I vehemently rejected Brücke's reaction as an insult to the dead, but I did not forget him. I wondered whether he succeeded in suppressing his inner anguish and in banishing his son not just from talk but from thought. Brücke's stern figure represented one extreme possibility, alien, but with a strength that I respected. He joined Mrs John Dewey and Philip Woolf in the gallery of archtypical mourners I had begun to assemble.

I adapted Hannah Arendt's phrase 'the banality of evil', which, whatever its original aptness or tact, conveyed the dismaying sense of disproportion that I felt in Sarah's death. A lack of proportion between trivial brief accidents and omissions and their vast devastating consequences. Even if I ignore the commonplace human failures that may have contributed to her death, and see it as brought about by a proliferating invasion of bacteria, that also seems an utterly inadequate cause for the annihilation of a loved and sturdy child and the destruction of a long and promising life. The banality of tragedy. Disproportion, I learned, is a basic reality of human life.

Two elegies by women, Caitlin Thomas and Anne Philipe, included thoughts and reactions that were often close to mine, although each mourned the death, not of a child, but of a husband. Caitlin Thomas's punchy language gave me several graphic and enduring phrases. On the complexity of mourning:

> I… go on daftly half waiting for him to come back when I know he cannot; but it is not a bit of good for reason to tell me that, it cannot stop the wanting so badly, reasonable or not; and where can I put it, what can I do with it. It is not a chasm, it is an enormous fruit cake, of wanting.

And on work as the only anodyne:

> … the necessity of picking up the humdrum tools yourself; brush, broom, shovel or pencil; and fashioning an object out of your own muddied dregs; even if it is no more than a fumbled one-eyed potato.

A succession of lucky chances lead me to Anne Philipe's meditation on the death from cancer of her husband Gérard Philipe. I happened on an extract in an Australian women's magazine, and then spotted the book in Cheshire's basement bookshop, in Melbourne where one could often search in vain for a book recently published in London. I have read her sad but controlled story of Gerard's illness, death and funeral many times, finding observations that I shared.

> Bang your head against the walls, scream, turn to stone, behave as though nothing had happened, bite, pray, revolt, accept, it changes nothing.

Obvious! But looking back over thirty years, I can see that

coming to understand grief is often coming to know (to 'really know') what you already know, and a means to that end is repeating in words, and finding in the words of others, many times over, what is plainly evident, yet constantly rediscovered with incredulous astonishment. I was still a long way from 'really knowing' this particular truth.

Caitlin Thomas's *Leftover Life to Kill,* and Ann Philipe's *No Longer than a Sigh,* are out of print and in danger of being forgotten under an avalanche of new books, but they should remain known as classics of grief.

Just as I became furious with friends who failed to offer their condolences, and equally with those who said the wrong thing, so I reacted with anger and scorn to writers whose attitudes jarred on new sensitivities. Phyllis McGinley, for example, whose deft and gently satirical verse about children and families I discovered in Camberwell. I copied out half a dozen poems, of which these lines are a sample:

> I love my daughters with a love unfailing,
> I love them healthy and I love them ailing…
> I love them gentle or inclined to mayhem
> But I love them warmest after eight-thirty a.m.
> Oh, the peace like heaven
> That wraps me around,
> Say at eight-thirty-seven,
> When they're schoolroom-bound
> With the last glove mated
> And the last scarf tied

> With the pigtail plaited
> With the pincurl dried,
> And the egg disparaged
> And the porridge sneered at,
> And the last night's comics furtively peered at…

The salutary ambivalence and rueful insight of a mother whose children are robustly alive! Which could even, I was later able to acknowledge, amuse a mother with one surviving child. But then I rejected her wit with contempt, as superficial, unappreciative of the miracle of childhood and the blessed gift of parenthood, cynically playing to the gallery, in every way damned. And even more upsetting:

> A mother's hardest to forgive.
> Life is the fruit she longs to hand you
> Ripe on a plate. And while you live,
> Relentlessly she understands you.

My condemnation sprang from envy. Life *was* the fruit I longed to hand her, and I still yearned to be that bountiful goddess. Only the mother of a living child, perhaps already adolescent, could be sufficiently detached to see her own intrusive generosity through a daughter's (or a son's) resentful eyes.

I heard insults, too, from Colette, writing in *Le Fanal Bleu* about her first sight of the actress Marguerite Moreno, who was seated in a sunlit room, nursing a handsome blonde infant son.

This magnificent child, whose birth had almost cost his frail mother her life, this luminous child died of meningitis before he was three, after fighting against death with a strength already that of a man. Few of us remember that he briefly existed. And I believe that Moreno – the beautiful austere name chosen by Marguerite Monceau – has rarely spoken of him except to contemporaries who, like me, had caught a glimpse of her transient, prematurely gifted son. ['Son fils fugitif, trop tôt prodigieux'.]

This was a piece I recalled often and ambivalently. I was grateful to Colette for evoking so vividly that child who died before his time, but I was indignant about the phrase 'trop tôt prodigieux'. What on earth could she mean by it? A waste for him to be so prodigious, since he died? That he should have waited to see whether he would survive before flourishing his precocity? Whatever she meant, her words dismiss the handsome blond child with flaunted virtuosity. 'Trop tôt prodigieux' focussed my anger at all those who view the death of a child too lightly, including for the moment Colette.

But I read and studied and knew equally by heart, the brief passages in Colette's journals about the birth of her daughter, and her wry comments on her own maternal propensities or lack of them. Colette was of an earlier generation and a different culture to mine; I could not produce her magisterial generalizations; but when I first started wondering how to write about Sarah there were very few first-hand accounts of becoming a mother. I learned through my differences from Colette, or Colette's public version of herself. If ever I entertained any fleeting attraction to the fantasy of immortality, it was banished by reading Swift's account of the Struldbruggs, the wretched immortals of Laputa.

> When they come to fourscore years, which is reckoned the extremity of living in this country, they had not only all the follies and infirmities of other old men, but many more which arose from the dreadful prospect of never dying. They were not only opinionative, peevish, covetous, morose, vain, talkative; but uncapable of friendship, and dead to all natural affection… At ninety they lose their teeth and hair; they have at that age no distinction of taste, but eat and drink whatever they can get, without relish or appetite. The diseases they were subject to still continue without increasing or diminishing. In talking, they forget the common appellation of things, and the names of persons, even of those who are their nearest friends and relations. For the same reason, they never can amuse themselves with reading, because their memory will not serve to carry them from the beginning of a sentence to the end; and by this defect, they are deprived of the only entertainment whereof they might otherwise be capable…

FIRST QUESTIONS

Camo Jackson recommended an anthology of modern European poetry, *The Poem Itself*, edited by Stanley Burnshaw. A wonderful book. Burnshaw wants us to read foreign poetry in its original language, even if we know it very imperfectly. Verse translation merely produces English poems, and probably not very good ones. He asked scholars of various European languages to choose poems they particularly admired, and to provide literal prose translations and whatever commentaries might help in their appreciation. For me, he is highly successful in this aim. *The Poem Itself* is one of the books I would least like to have missed. Through it I came to know Valéry, Hofmannsthal, Rilke, Brecht, Unamuno and Salinas, to name only those who spoke most clearly to my grief.

Paul Valéry gave me an essential phrase. 'Le Cimetière Marin', his meditation in the cemetery of Sète on a hillside overlooking a dazzling sea, is a magnificent poem which I don't fully understand, even with the help of Burnshaw's translator, but some images and phrases have stuck with me, most persistently two lines, and from them three words.

> Les morts cachés sont bien dans cette terre
> Qui les réchauffe et sèche leur mystère.
> The hidden dead lie easy in that earth
> Which warms their bones. and dries their mystery.

'Sèche leur mystère' is the phrase I adopted. Mystery is the vital core of being, the unique personhood of each human individual, which does not immediately disappear from our awareness when they die. We continue to think of our loved dead as centres of vital and unknowable possibility, as if they were alive but absent. We still want to honour, love and protect them. By contrast, most of those who died long ago have lost this mystery. They are corpses, bones, names, enjoyably-melancholy wraiths, tragic or comic figures. Valéry wrote of this drying-up of mystery as beneficent. His words defined that eventuality, but I rejected it as utterly impossible for her and for me. Again and again in the journals I insist that to recall her is to see a person abounding in energy, hope and promise whose mystery is still vibrant.

I repeated, also, lines from a poem by Bertold Brecht, not in Burnshaw although he lead me to it, 'Grosser Dankchoral', (Thanksgiving Chorale) – a hymn of praise for mortality, decay and anonymity.

> Lobet von Hertzen das schlechte Gedächtnis des Himmels!
> Und das er nicht
> Weiss euren Nam noch Gesicht
> Niemand weiss, dass ihr noch da seid.
>
> Lobet die Kälte, die Finsternis und das Verderben!
> Schauet hinan:
> Es kommet nicht auf euch an
> Und ihr könnt unbesorgt sterben.
>
> Praise from your heart the appalling memory of Heaven!
> It does not know

FIRST QUESTIONS

Either your name or your face,
No-one knows if you are still there.

Praise ye the cold, the darkness and the corruption!
Look beyond;
It cares for you not a jot
And you can die without worry.

An odd addiction! Despite my rudimentary German, I repeated these lines to myself for years, finding in them some sort of comfort. I don't think I saw them as a commentary on Sarah's death, rather as a detached general truth. I haven't come across many celebrations of the finality of death. Perhaps we need more.

Most of these readings, when not furiously indignant, seem sane and sensible, part of a rational if painful attempt to reshape my view of the world so as to encompass her death. The lesson of each is still easy to understand. That is not so of a passage from Dostoyevsky's *Letters from the Underworld* which haunted me persistently for a long while. Less a text than a dramatic situation. I didn't memorise Dostoyevsky's words, but I carried around with me an atmosphere, and an image, that of the Underground Man, resentfully hostile to the entire world and its rules and values. He is not, he snarls, the sort of person who 'goes straight to his goal as a mad bull charges with lowered crest; and nothing but a stone wall will stop him.' On the contrary, *he* is not going stop merely because his way is blocked by a stone wall.

What stone wall, do you say? Why the stone wall constituted of the laws of nature, of the deductions of learning, and of the science of mathematics... 'Pardon us,' so these people bawl, ' but you simply cannot refute what we tell you. Twice two make four; Nature does not ask your leave for that; she has nothing to do with your wishes on the subject, no matter whether you approve of her laws or not. You must just take her as she is, and with her, her results. A wall still remains a wall.' – and so forth, and so forth... Good Lord! What have I to do with the laws of Nature, or with arithmetic, when all the time those laws and the formula that twice two makes four do not meet with my acceptance? Of course, I am not going to beat my head against a wall if I have not the requisite strength to do so; yet I am not going to accept that wall merely because I have run up against it, and have no means to knock it down.

I seized on this furiously self-righteous rejection of reality, and adopted as my own the image of a wall which I refused to recognise. I didn't analyse or explore the meanings of the wall, or discuss it in any of the diaries I kept at the time. I didn't need to write about it because I identified myself unquestioningly with the Underground Man. Her death was a stark reality, an adamantine wall that had suddenly blocked our path, changing the future for all of us. But her sudden annihilation was so monstrously alien to my past happiness and future expectations, for myself but even more for her, that despite knowing that it had irrevocably happened, I could not accept it. The Underground Man's logic insisted that I should not. I remained committed to this justification of intransigence, even while I struggled to find my way through or over that terrible wall. I used to expostulate to myself, 'Why should I recognise that wall? What is it to me? Mere brute fact, nothing to do with my love and longing for her, or with her vitality and beauty and transcendent deserts.' Defiance that seemed unanswerable.

Dostoyevsky's Underground Man became a focus for the irrationality of grief, the need to deny and to hope, that lay dormant in the first few weeks after she died, but then emerged to exert its power, multifariously, for many years to come. The Underground Man was for a time my model and my companion. And then at some point, long before the impulse to protest finally flickered out, his hold over me dissolved so completely that I could no longer quite understand what it had been.

III

A Diary of Grief
1965-1966

About a year after Sarah died, I began to keep a new record, the Diary of Grief ('DG' for short), which grew out of those long therapeutic sessions of undisciplined writing. Some of the ideas and observations that turned up were so surprising, illogical and unlike the person I imagined myself to be, that I decided to keep a separate record of them, more concisely and deliberately written. The Diary of Grief soon expanded in scope and became the Diaries, which I have continued ever since. But sporadically. There were periods when I felt acutely involved with questions of life and death and her death and memory, and wanted to explore them in writing. Between times, the concerns of on-going life were more demanding, and the Diary of Grief was neglected.

I wrote the preceding chapters retrospectively, from memory and scattered notes. What follows is a contemporaneous record drawn from the Diary of Grief. It is only a fraction of the whole, which is far too voluminous and repetitive to share in its entirety. The chosen entries are separated by intervals of time varying from days to weeks, months and even years. Individually, they remain as first written. I have occasionally added a later comment (in italics), but for the most part I have resisted the temptation to seem wiser or more perceptive than I was.

Deep within myself, when I think of Sarah I expect to be with her again. I think of her, and think, I long to be with her and I *will* be. The wish is so strong that it creates a fleeting expectation.

Just a year ago we went to Vaughn Springs, and she and I climbed a hillside pocked with the hollows and vestigial walls of a once-prosperous gold-digging town. Later, in the fading evening light, we visited a koala sanctuary overlooking a wide empty plain, and she called to the sleeping koalas, 'Come down, I want to see you! Come down bear!' I look up on the map the towns we visited the next day, yearning for that lost freshness and beauty and liveliness, for the happiness of being together, for the two children's love for each other, and for their energy. While we waited outside the Bendigo Art Gallery for Mama and Erwin to emerge, they climbed onto the parapet of the steps and jumped into my arms 'one after the other'.

Other people have their tragedies too, but mine is for me unique, unalterable, and impossible to accept calmly. That is what I spend hours trying to do, to accept it so that I get moments of relief. And they do happen. I remember that in the first days, acute misery was sometimes replaced by intervals of exhausted dreaminess in which Sarah's death ceased to lacerate just because I was so tired. Now the relief comes when I get absorbed in some other activity, even something as mundane as ordering clothes.

I saw a little girl on the beach at Point Lonsdale in the summer, suntanned and wearing only a brief pair of pants. She could have been Sarah. I watched her with almost the same tenderness, and thought – there is more grace and beauty in the curve of her back as she plays on the sand than in all my memories of Sarah, or that I can evoke by writing about her.

My love, my beauty, my Sarah, how can we ever answer our despair except with the knowledge that your lot was better than some and worse than others? Which is what one can say about anyone. Luckier than some and less lucky than others.

I continue to repeat this formula, with variations, about her and about myself. Sometimes it seems to sum up everything that can be said, and to provide what little consolation is possible.

Erwin recalled that once, in France, we had seen miniature cyclamen growing in the woods. We discussed where it could have been. He said, 'Sarah was with us. But then I always think it was with Sarah when I remember anything pretty.'

This morning a sudden memory brought a new flash of disbelief that she, so young, beautiful and vital, could die. I saw us on a country outing late last summer, walking up a steep track through trees towards a fire-tower. Sarah, with jubilant intensity, picked up some chips of wood and an empty cigarette packet. That's all – except for the feeling of joy and completeness at being together on a beautiful day in the freshness of the bush, and with a new pleasure in store for Mama and the children. We planned to have an Australian chop picnic and then dress the children in their pyjamas before starting home, so that they would fall asleep in the car and we could carry them straight to bed. Sarah was lively and absorbed in everything, as always; when we stopped the car, she ran off 'to investigate', and I noticed that although she still danced in a circle around us, its radius was increasing.

But the idyllic picnic place I had chosen turned out to be littered with paper and beer cans, and stinking with half-buried crayfish remains. We drove around looking for another site, arriving eventually at Emerald lake. By then it was getting late, the few picnickers who remained drove away while we prepared supper, a cold wind blew up, and a huge hoarding announcing a subdivision stared at us across the lake – the nostalgic countryside of my childhood turning into suburbia. We ate hurriedly, and the children remained awake all the way home. A day of cherished memory despite ending with a whimper.

Since Sarah's death I have been mad, and I think I always will be. Meaning? That my view of reality and my scale of values are distorted – different from other people's and not rational. Her life and death overshadow everything else – the interests of friends and their work, the war in Vietnam. And not just in importance for me, but in absolute importance. I can't get absorbed in discussion or thinking about anything, large or small, for long, because the only thing that matters is Sarah and reflecting about her death. I can't see the world for the immense looming bulk of her death.

Fragments of an inner monologue that has gone on for fifteen months now:

In front of Myers, 'This is where we looked at the Cinderella windows at Christmas. This place is still here and real. So she must be real too.'

At an exhibition of Nolan paintings, 'How can I admire and rejoice at his achievement, when she who brought infinitely greater rejoicing is dead?'

Preparing for a trip to Sydney, 'You mean you are calmly going to Sydney without her and staying in the same motel as if nothing had happened? Walking up the street where we saw the fire engine?'

Driving down Spring Street, hot and tired and glad to be on my way home. I admire the pale-blue sky streaked with cloud, and think – 'She will never see a sky like that.' But this time I note the fact without distress, perhaps because once before, descending the same hill, I had thought with searing anguish that she would never see the piled-up clouds in a sky, that day, of fierce intensity.

Sydney. Passing high above Circular Quay and looking down on the harbour and the docks from which, once, the liners departed for Europe and the troopships for two world wars, I had a vision of Sarah's death as a leave-taking, a parting of momentous inevitability, and sadness beyond words or tears. She stood on the deck of a ship which was pulling slowly away, watching me with a sad and solemn expression on her beautiful child's face, while the strip of dark glassy water between us widened inexorably. The great powerful ship would carry her further and further away, and neither of us could prevent it. I have known such departures. When I was a child, my mother sailed for England more than once, while we children held streamers and waved goodbye; and I myself, as a young graduate, left Australia from this same Circular Quay to study at Columbia University, aware that I was leaving home for good.

At Rushcutter's Bay. Daniel plays in the swimming pool, just as Sarah did. I stare at the windows of the rooms we had two years ago with her. However hard I try to make them look like the others, I don't succeed. They are ours and hers, and they look more alive. *She* is still there.

Constantly I repeat, 'It isn't right; we shouldn't be here without her' – the protest I have been making for fifteen months. Astonishment that all this should exist and she not. It should have died with her. She is not here to watch, talk with, care for. But she's not dead. We don't just get on with what can still be done, without her. She still has an active role in our lives. A ghost, a lively vivid ghost.

It would be bearable if I could just think, 'This is my lot, which I must simply accept.' To face so terrible a reality and learn to endure it would be a challenge . But it is also her lot, and that is unassimilable. There is no triumph in learning to bear her lot.

I behave like a ham actor, pleading, with a melodramatic display of pathos, for something impossible, appealing to someone who isn't there. It's absurd and it is what I still do much of the time. 'But see how beautiful she was, how happy we were!' in the hope that a non-existent heart will soften, a non-existent decision be revoked.

I have been sorting Daniel's clothes, putting some away for the summer, and others that are outgrown into a box for giving away. I found things of Sarah's too, some still where she left them before she died. It is time I gave them away, or at least some of them, perhaps the bride doll that was her asked-for birthday present. Reluctantly I choose a pair of gloves for the give-away box, but the rest go into storage, packed with the same care as Daniel's, as if she will need them again.

I realise suddenly that, without conscious intention everything is still here, so that she could return and carry on her life as if she had never been away. Dan wears her green rain jacket and some vests and pyjamas, but they could be given back. Some of her toys remain in the playroom, the more vulnerable are in the linen cupboard. It was only a few weeks ago that I threw out the broken candles from her birthday cake, wrapping them thickly in newspaper and putting them furtively in the rubbish bin.

I think of the bereaved who have deliberately kept everything as it was. An aging couple, friends of Mama's, once showed me the room in their cramped flat which had been their daughter's: dolls propped on the bed, nursery pictures on the wall, everything left unchanged since she died fifteen years earlier. What could be the motive except a phantom hope that their child might return?

In my ceaseless preoccupation with Sarah, I pursue two impossibilities –to restore her to life, or to see her death as somehow fair or just. How am I to live if it can be neither cancelled nor accepted? The answer is obvious – only by turning my energy to other things. Gradually, I suppose, that is what I do. But it is hard to understand even for myself, why such an obvious necessity is so difficult.

Shortly after Sarah died, I read a passage in *Friends Apart*, Philip Toynbee's memoir of his friends Esmond Romilly and Jasper Ridley, who were both killed in the war.

By now, ten years after the death of Jasper, I have had time enough in which to accept the fact that their lives have ended, for themselves and for all of us. I believe that I have made this difficult act of credulity, for death is now firmly stamped across their faces whenever I bring them back to mind. That they are now dead seems as much their quality, their portion, as that they were once alive, once did this and that, said this and that. Their everlasting absence is as clear to me as their presence was once clear.

I rejected in fury that phrase 'death is stamped across their faces'. I too believed I had accepted the fact of Sarah's death, but when I thought of her it was of someone vibrantly alive. Death was not stamped on *her* face. I thought that Toynbee was implying that his friends' early deaths had been foreordained, marking them even while they lived. That misinterpretation was part of what I violently denied. Sarah's death was brought about by an unforeseen and unforeseeable tangle of events. No shadow of impending death had fallen on her life, and no shadow would fall on my memory of her.

I returned often to Toynbee's brutal phrase, denying, criticizing, grudgingly accepting. It echoed through an incident years later. I had applied for a passport for Daniel, because we would be returning to London from Majorca separately. I asked the Australian passport office in London if I also would need a new passport to replace our shared one, and was told that they could simply change the photograph, so I provided a new one of myself. But when, the day before we were due to leave, I collected the passports, I discovered in mine the photograph of the two of us with Daniel's face obliterated by a heavy black bar. Death stamped across his face! I could not have travelled with such a document. But, I was told, it would take three days for me to get a new passport. At that I broke into such a torrent of outrage and anger and accusation and despair that the official agreed to provide one within two hours. It is one of the few times I have won a victory over bureaucracy, but my triumph was tempered by shame at having pleaded Sarah's death in order to gain it.

We went to Williamstown for the first time since that dark drizzly Sunday when we were there with her. Today was still and sunny and the bay was sprinkled far and wide with ships. Again I broke a spell and walked on hallowed ground. Awareness of her absence clung most densely around a little Victorian drinking-fountain with a curly canopy. Why that? Williamstown, now a forlorn backwater, was a thriving port in the early days of the colony, and on that gloomy Sunday I had been searching for nostalgic survivals. Little remains; the fountain had been one of the few pleasing sights, and the focus of my greatest appreciation – and it is near the Ladies where I had taken Sarah – the focus her greatest interest.

If I write the book about her, and then DG, and perhaps a third I have begun to think about, then through her death I will have gained an aim for my own life, for which I have always been searching. Already I have the conviction that I have found it. I don't feel smug about it. Not good coming of evil, but good and evil mixed in everything. If I could change the past, I would immediately throw away this finding of myself in return for Sarah alive.

During the last week I have had attacks of grief so sharp and blinding that I can't understand what I have been feeling for eighteen months. I know that I have been preoccupied with thoughts of Sarah and often in misery, but I couldn't conceivably have felt this intensity of sorrow for so long.

I am driven to work by pain. When she was alive, I frittered away my time pleasantly. If I produce a book about her, and then perhaps another, it will be through trying to escape the misery that has stupefied me for days past. Today I have spent two hours writing, and the result is to make me feel so much more cheerful, so much more ready to accept that Sarah is dead, that my thoughts veer off onto a shopping expedition in town, and a trip to Venice some time in the future. Venice will always hold part of her life. We were there when I was pregnant, before anyone knew but Erwin and me. In the mornings, I used to sit at a café by the Grand Canal with an unread book, contemplating the sunlight dancing on the water, while Erwin visited the Accademia.

A DIARY OF GRIEF

I'm trying out a new chant to push away despair: 'IT IS, IT IS, IT IS! Her death IS!'

At Lorne for two days. Sarah is in my mind even when I'm in the surf. I want to save up experiences for her: sun on a leaden sea, mauve paint on the red wood of a pile of new fish boxes. To note them and store them away. Not for Daniel, who is alive; for Sarah who is dead.

Camo said, 'The first thing to remember is that you're not the only one.' But for me, just IT IS!

IV

A Homecoming
1966-1970

During this time we had been living in Melbourne although our home was in London, where our children had been born. We had returned to Australia in January 1962 to see my mother, who had cancer, and to show her the children, Daniel, then a baby, and Sarah, three and a half. The visit had lasted much longer than anticipated. because I became involved in negotiations over the future of the family business. After my mother's death, we had settled into the back half of the rambling suburban house in which I had grown up. My father continued to occupy the front half and Mama, my mother-in-law, had joined us when it became obvious that we would not soon be returning home. The business discussions had been prolonged and sometimes acrimonious, but by the middle of 1966 we had completed a reorganisation, and I had sold my share to my cousin Peter.

In September we left Melbourne to return to London. We had looked forward to the journey home as an escape and the promise of some renewal of joy. Our airtickets gave us a generous mileage allowance and unlimited stopovers, and we planned to stay in Hong Kong, Cambodia, Bangkok, Greece and Vienna.

The journey was indeed enjoyable and full of splendid sights, but also heavy with grief. I was aware all the time of her capricious absence. She should have been with us. Watching the junks in Hong Kong harbour, walking down a mountain road in Cambodia and coming suddenly upon monkeys swinging through the treetops, contemplating the silent grandeur of Delphi, enjoying coffee and pflaumentorte in a Viennese cafe, I was also thinking of her. There was no opportunity for long sessions at the typewriter, but I scribbled a few notes.

Hong Kong
Erwin and I agree that the Chinese children remind us often of Sarah. I compare their relaxed limbs, their tawny skins, their cheerful liveliness. Erwin said, 'It's the dark eyes and long eyelashes. And they often have wide nostrils, like she did.' I think of her lovely nostrils with longing.

Holding Daniel's hot little hand, I think, Is he feverish? No, it's just the heat of the day. And I imagine myself holding Sarah's hand protectively, while she gets more and more feverish, until she dies, while I am still smugly holding her soft burning hand.

Young, cheerful and competent Chinese shoemaker to Erwin: 'You have one son. I have one son and one daughter.' After he had left the room Erwin broke into sobs. I don't have tears, but perhaps brood over her death more obsessively.

Still this endless searching, wrangling, experimenting and circling around obstinate false beliefs: Somewhere she *is*, abandoned, frightened and bewildered, needing our help. I am on the brink of discovering how to bring her back. Someone so beautiful, joyful, growing and exploring with such intensity, *can't* die; if I appeal forcefully enough to some obscure authority, it will relent and she will return. Endless inner debate that is at the same time hopeful and despairing.

Phnom Penh
Two days ago, swimming in the warm sea at Kep, I thought yet again, 'How she would have loved it!' And then: 'Not she would have enjoyed it! She did enjoy precisely this, water and swimming.' Now I try to counter the stab of regret by telling myself 'She did know it, we shared it.'

Learn to hold a feeling of the beauty of her life like water cupped in my hands, carefully. Any jerk or shock and it will spill over into searing grief. I have often felt this.

A HOMECOMING

In the plane between Bangkok and New Delhi
'I can't even love her now. There is no Sarah to love.' For a moment, flushed with the experiences of the last weeks, I accept.

Athens
I turn for days now around the problem of seeing her calmly as a being who lived for five years and then died, instead of as someone living an absent, perhaps suspended, life. The last two years and the many still to come have no existence for her. Useless torture to play with the might-have-been. Learn not to. Yet even Freud did not dismiss such thoughts: 'Today my daughter Sophie would have been 36.'

Delphi
Walking past small shops hung with bright hand-loomed woollens and fur pelts, Erwin commented: 'How Sarah would have loved this. She would have adored stroking the furs, and I would certainly have had to buy her one.'

Crete
I go over the reasons for setting myself, seriously, with determination, the task of learning to live for the present and future, without her: I can't do anything for her; no matter how fervently I desire to help her and give to her, she isn't aware of my longing; not just pointless, but painful and exhausting for me; my image of her becomes less and

less alive, pale, uninvigorating, unsustaining, tedious. None of this is new, even for me. What is hard to express is my conviction of making a new discovery each time such reflections return.

Athens again
A terrible desolation engulfs me when I think of the moment when the darkness of death overcame Sarah. I struggle to regain the joy that she existed, which for moments I have felt today. Cecily said, 'There's nothing that can be done.' She immediately understood that essential lesson. For me it is very long to learn.

There are no notes from Vienna. The drive into the city, past sombre apartment blocks, under a leaden sky, was a melancholy reintroduction to northern Europe, but our days in Vienna were busy and cheerful. I recall a room overlooking a domed baroque church, visits to the Kunsthistorisches Museum, mainly for Erwin, while I went to the Natural History Museum with Daniel, and to the Opera for me, while Erwin babysat, and sending off a telegram at midnight to Klaus and Julie announcing our arrival in London next day by Pan Am One.

We returned to the flat from which the four of us had set out in the first heady days of our existence as a family. For a second time we came home without her to a house filled with her presence. The Diary continued.

A HOMECOMING

Taboos on places. I approach Holland Park, where I walked last with a confident and loved not-yet-three Sarah, this time reluctantly and miserably, with heavy feet. I haven't yet been back to Sainsbury's, where she knew all the checkout girls and sat on the cash desk talking to them while I trundled round collecting groceries. "Where's Sarah?" they would to ask if she were not with me. In Australia I never returned to the Colosimos' fruit stall near the Glenferrie market, never once after she died. If I had to walk past, I averted my eyes from the effusive Sicilian couple, refusing to recognise them.

Why the taboos? To begin with, the obvious answer is true – it is a painful reminder of loss. The little fishpond in Holland Park looked exactly as it did five years ago, setting up a tense vibration – she is here, she is not here. Then there is the tenacious belief, which I identified long ago after a sudden desertion, that as long as you don't go back to a scene of vanished happiness, the past lives on there unchanged, he, she, is still there, waiting until next time. Different again with the Colosimos. I shunned a public display of defeat, especially painful in front of a couple whose continuing good fortune we once shared. They have a little boy, dull, we thought, in comparison with our own lively two, and we used to buy our weekend vegetables in an atmosphere of shared child-worship.

My face in the mirror, a bereaved, lined face. I see it, but I don't yet acknowledge that it is me – still don't recognise myself as someone irreversibly scarred by fate.

Forgetting Sarah. Inevitable and unverifiable. I can at any moment summon up an image of her as vivid as if I had seen her yesterday, but is it remembered or invented? I felt so confident that this companion-ghost is her that I was utterly astonished when I noticed just now that I think of her as older, wiser, more continuously in communion with me than my vanished five-year-old daughter ever could have been.

One pleasure I can no longer describe – the mornings when she came into my bed. What did we do, how did we lie, what did we talk about? Daniel this morning brought his fish book for me to read, laughing when I mocked its pretentious language: 'Surfacing for air, a rich-hued Siamese fighting-fish has just expelled bubbles of vitiated air…' We laugh, he asks me to 'read it funny' again, I do, and explain the meanings and replace the derided words by simpler ones. Then he puts his cold feet against my leg, and lies on top of me, joyfully and suggestively, claiming that he needs to be kept warm.

I can't recall such a scene with Sarah, yet from her very first days I accepted being woken early, although before she was born I had often slept until late. I welcomed her without complaining because I loved her, and because the thought of rejecting her joyful early-morning advances was more painful than my reluctant emergence from sleep. When I hear of young children who never wake their parents, but play quietly on their own, my heart shrinks. Sometimes there is a comment on how clever the parents have been to discourage early morning visits, sometimes it is suggested that the children have adopted this habit entirely on their own. I don't believe either of these. Montessori, whom I read only after she died, is right, parents contrive to defend themselves against their children's love so as not to give up their own convenience.

Daniel's first day at school. He takes my hand companionably on the way, clinging to me ('You can teach me, Mum'), but I see myself as I will appear to him in 20 years time, old, unglamorous, half-pitied and almost wholly despised. I feel my face becoming soft and slack like my mother's, not taut and smooth as it has been until almost now. Yet despite this forecast of rejection, these days have brought a degree of healing through busyness with external problems – new schools, doctors, re-organising the flat.

Phone call from Margaret suggesting she take us to the country tomorrow. The weather is lovely but I am in bed with a temperature so must refuse. These repeated invitations must be her way of showing sympathy for Sarah's death. She did not write and has never spoken of it. I imagine Sarah's beauty in the sunny countryside as I lie in bed, and feel a soft hopeless sorrow near to tears. It occurs to me that the value of sympathy is in encouraging this only possible release from grief, that of hopeless tears. But still they do not flow.

A visit from friends we have not seen since before we went to Australia. They are encouraging to Daniel and flattering to us about him, but I am icily aware that there is no mention of Sarah. They force us to behave as if she were dead. And what else do I expect? She is dead. Then – they force us to behave as if she never lived.

I have found another archetype of mourning, Ommanney's cook, in the memoir which F.D. Ommanney, a fisheries expert, wrote about his three years at Hong Kong University. When the husband of his servant Ah Yok was killed in a street accident, Ah Yok, her face 'puckered with grief and tears', brought the news to her employer.

> The next morning she called me as usual. She had loosened her hair and for three days wore it thus, spread about her shoulders like a cloak down to her waist. For three days she mourned, not in silence and privately as we should, but with loud unabashed weeping so that all the world should behold her grief and share her sorrow. Loud sobs and at times blubbering added her tears to the washing up. They mingled with the cooking. On the third evening, which was a Sunday, I decided I had had enough of grief and began to wonder how much longer she would mourn aloud. I went to Joe's Bar for the evening. Before I went I asked her how much longer. I dare say I spoke more brusquely than I meant to.

'Tomollow finish, Master,' she replied, with dignity and humility.

The next day Ah Yok was herself again. The mourning was over. She had bound up her hair again and put a gilt pin in it. She had put on a clean white tunic and smiled once more. During the rest of the time I knew her she never again referred to her bereavement, though occasionally to its consequences.

This behaviour is no more a possible model for me than is Ernst Brücke's, but I think of them both often, with a mixture of puzzlement and admiration.

Trying to recall the name of a deserted mining town we visited in winter sunshine on a trip to Bendigo, I get out a map of Victoria. As I trace the road we took that day, I am shaking with terror. The pain of recall, the paralysing pain and fear of trying to write about a paradise whose image is scarred by knowledge of her death. I want to write of joy unstained by later grief.

Today a boy of 10 was killed when a sports pavilion collapsed in a storm; the teacher had ordered the class to take shelter and he was the first to reach it. I collect such accidents. Killed on the way to school when a brick wall heeled over, buried while playing on a sandpile, hanged in the half-open window of the family car, run over by an ice-cream van. Sudden, unpredictable, grotesque deaths, which I need in order to demonstrate what I know already – that this world is one in which children, in which anyone, can die at any moment, through no-one's immediate fault. It is a truth I need to hear repeated over and over again.

I see myself as a trodden-on beetle lying on its back with half its legs crushed, jerking feebly and unable to turn right-side up; the only thing to do is put it out of its misery. And sometimes I am Sonya, who had a brief hour of happiness driving through the snow with her cousin Nicholas at Christmas, before her blossoming was aborted by the realisation that Nicholas could never marry her. 'She is a sterile flower, you know, like some strawberry blossoms,' Natasha said. In Sarah's lifetime I flowered, not just with love and happiness, but with confidence, strength and purpose. Now I feel shrivelled.

The push-chair is white enamel with a red seat, and shiny like new. The young woman in a tweed coat and little fur hat, who answered my advertisement in the *Kensington Post*, tells me she has four children. I hear myself saying calmly, 'You see it folds down so that it is quite flat. My daughter was a great sleeper.' Vividness of Sarah and the chestnut trees by the canal that sunny May when I bought the pusher because I was going to take my one-year-old daughter to the country for a few days.

A HOMECOMING

I looked up 'Childbirth' in the subject index at the library. No books on childbirth, but I found two memoirs about dying children. Borrowed *The Story of Gabrielle* by Catherine Gabrielson – a mother's account of the illness and death of her nine-year-old daughter from cancer. It is vividly and sparely written, and I read it with intense empathy. One function for such memoirs – to enable us to live through the parts of our lives that have been skimped. Sarah's death flashed upon us and was over before we knew it was happening. Reading this book I can imagine living through and sharing her dying. But I question its ending, which follows a description of Gabby's funeral:

> It was a beautiful occasion, light and wondrous like you. But why am I telling you all this – you must have been there, as you are never far now. Otherwise, how would I have been able to walk away so flooded with the light of your strong and vibrant spirit, more able to live fully than ever before?

I don't doubt her mood of exaltation, but to end the book in this way suggests that it was permanent, and I am sceptical about that. She must have gone through, later, the same bewildering switches and repetitions, the same anger, protest, anguish and despair, as the rest of us.

A lovely early summer day, almost hot, the trees flaring wildly in their fresh green, a day such as I haven't known since our last summer here together, before we all went to

Australia. Renewed anguish and grief. Again the conviction that there is something I don't understand, a baffled sense of the instability of this terrible situation we are in, as if I've only got to find the right password and I will be back with her and Daniel, an unstricken family, in this unchanged leafy garden.

Oliffe Richmond told us about a fellow student at East Sydney Tech, a woman studying sculpture so that she could make a memorial to her son who had died in the war. He had been the rear turret gunner in an aircraft where there was no room for a parachute and he was supposed to crawl back to get it. Instead, he jumped hanging on to a mate, but couldn't hold on long enough. Oliffe laughed wryly during the telling. I see myself as that woman, trying, with no particular talent, to learn to write so that I can write her memorial.

'I live her death' – a phrase, mine, that I repeat often. Meaning that everything I experience, I see as an experience which she will never know. Everything. We were sitting in the kitchen with Klaus Loewald and his wife. Klaus told of visiting a German tavern and drinking white beer mixed with raspberry juice. 'It sounds terrible, and it was – terrible! But quite good too.' We laughed and suddenly I was stabbed by the recognition that she would never know the pleasure of sharing a mild joke with friends.

A HOMECOMING

Rarity of meditations on death by non-believers. Not on our own death, there are plenty of those, but on that of the beloved other. If there were more and better in existence, I wouldn't need to write.

About to visit the Ss. I feel a strong sense of deprivation at the knowledge that they won't mention her, will probably never speak of her again, ever. And I see that this is inevitable. But I wish it were the custom, after enquiries about the living, to speak of the dead. 'I hope your thoughts of Sarah are happy ones', or better, 'We wish Sarah could have been here too.'

I am glad of our choice of where to leave her ashes. I often picture the track in the mountains, miles from any habitation, thinly covered with snow that day, surrounded by spindly black tree-trunks, as the place where her life ended, a place that will remain undesecrated for many years, that carries none of the alien associations of a cemetery, but is hallowed by our visits with her: on one side the high valley where we picnicked and she reported seeing a wet-furred kangaroo move through the undergrowth; on the other side, the timber mill where the children played in a broken-down truck under a flowering wattle tree, while Erwin prowled around collecting the scraps of discarded metal from which he made his first sculptures.

Reading Shelley – various poems on his son William's death. Not especially moving, still less on the death of Clara or the others. The longest one on William breaks off when Shelley tries to speak of his spirit passing into flowers and grasses. As if that had seemed a consolation until he came to write, when it proved painfully inadequate. Not a consolation that has ever appealed to me, but it is what Anne Philipe told her children:

> I wanted our children to keep a luminous vision of you, and never be touched by that idea of the putrefaction of the body which pursued me for months… but I didn't want to say either that you were in the sky, since that's not what we believed. So I tried to link you with life. I said: he's been transformed, he has become two trees and some flowers. Bees crawl inside the flowers and make honey, and we eat the honey and that way everything begins all over.

Poignancy of revisited places. Some of the reluctance wears off when I remind myself that I am merely trying to protect an illusion, but such visits remain intensely moving, and sometimes happily so. Today I felt an uprush of thanksgiving as I drove towards Henley, where we were together soon after her first birthday. I had been feeling fed-up with confined domesticity and had impulsively fled with her to the country for a few days. We stopped in Henley for tea, a rest on the flight. I gazed peacefully at an ancient brick wall across the street glowing in the late-afternoon sunshine, and she drank a glass of milk, competently and unaided, to the admiration of other tea-drinking ladies.

I had booked a room in a country-house hotel nearby, and we spent a first night there, but the scenery was too domesticated for my mood – cow country! Next day we wandered on, ending up at Limpley Stoke near Bath, where Cecily joined us and she and I went for sunny morning walks while Sarah slept, in charge of the barmaid.

A review of Peter Nichols's play *A Day in the Death of Joe Egg*, about life with a grossly defective child. The reviewer quotes Camus: 'Everything begins with lucid indifference,' and continues;
> The lucid indifference which can see our misfortunes as truly absurd is rare and refreshing. Although television and magazines now present a huge variety of tragic situations using the hushed sad voices of people in church, the sane sound of laughter on such topics has, until recently, not been heard... You leave the theatre feeling in every way better for having shared the author's experience, and for having, as he also had, the sensibility to laugh.

I am sceptical about that 'better'. It helps me to know that others also suffer, but that's not particularly admirable. Joe Egg is not my child, and I share her parents' dilemmas only from a distance. I shift to my own situation, but the reviewer does too: 'An audience is made up of individual husbands, wives, parents and children puzzling over the unplayable hand they have been dealt.' I want to be a loving, protective, joyful, appreciative parent to my daughter and I can't because the unplayability of that hand is that she is dead. And I'm to laugh!

But no doubt eventually I do. At myself! Though not very mirthfully. In 1995 this long-past indignation prompts a wry cackle. It took me a very long time to understand that the recommended laughter is not at her, not at events, but at oneself.

I throw away another relic of her life – paper patterns for dresses for a two-year-old. But I put back into the cupboard the wrappings from her presents the Christmas before we left for Australia – brightly-coloured papers with drawings by Klaus and Erwin.

A letter from Sigmund Freud, written nine years after the death of his daughter Sophie, to his colleague Dr Binswanger, who had lost a son:
> It is the only way of perpetuating the love which we do not want to relinquish. My daughter who died would have been 36 years old today… Although we know that after such a loss the acute state of mourning will subside, we also know we shall remain inconsolable and will never find a substitute. No matter what may fill the gap, even if it be filled

completely, it nevertheless remains something else.

And actually this is how it should be.

We remain inconsolable and we want to remain inconsolable, despite admonitions to return fully to life, despite the intermittently attractive promise of eventually reaching a state of serene acceptance. I am glad to know this letter. Because it was from Freud, who legitimises that refusal by lending it his immense authority. And because he did not write in the rebarbative language of his own theories, but in the words of any sensitive and articulate person.

I still think of her all the time. Not true of course, but more nearly true than I would have thought possible before. Today, I drove out to the Chilterns and walked for three hours in quiet country suspended between autumn and winter. She was in my mind all the time, her death, my life without her, why I should find it so hard to counter the anguish that she died with rejoicing that she lived. Any sudden moment of beauty – cabbages in a field, sun shining on yellow beech-leaves – seemed to promise continuing life for her. I expect her, I demand her. Childish omnipotence. But the reaction to remembering that she is dead is not childish yells of rage, but a desolate emptiness.

Of course I am really mad. This incessant preoccupation with Sarah is a form of madness, a living in an unreal world. Nothing to be done about it – except write that book about her, the one real-life thing I can do. And for that I have to come out of this dream atmosphere into the everyday. Writing is work and requires plain hard thinking. Nothing else to be done, not for her, not even connected with her. I can't talk to anyone; they would all be repelled or embarrassed by my continued absorption.

One of the most tenacious of my exemplary mourners is Aunt Julia, whom I encountered in an autobiography. Unusually, I didn't at the time copy out the bits that impressed me, nor make any note of the author and title of the book. Aunt Julia's son died young, and the memory of his death dominated her life, providing the standard by which she judged everyone: 'He was so good to me when the boy died.' I have tried to find Aunt Julia again, without success, but I have now come across her like in the person of Mary McCarthy's Grandmother Preston in *Memories of a Catholic Girlhood*, endlessly mourning the death of her daughter in the flu epidemic of 1919. 'Wilful and selfish', Mary McCarthy calls her grief. 'I see my grandmother, bearing her loss like an affront, stubborn and angry, refusing to speak not only to individual persons but to life itself, which had wounded her by taking her daughter away.' I have often admonished myself by recalling Aunt Julia, but Grandmother Preston is such a dominating figure, and so convincingly situated in her time and place and station in life by Mary McCarthy that I don't identify with her.

A HOMECOMING

Driving through the park, looking at the rain-drenched trees whose leaves are not yet thick enough to hide the outline of the branches, I remember driving there while Sarah was alive, not always with her but thinking of her, often on an errand for her, rejoicing in the beauty of the park because it was the world into which she would grow up. Today, suddenly it was this optimistic, appreciative self whom I mourned. 'Never glad confident morning again.'

I have been reading Maurice Goudeket's account in *The Delights of Growing Old*, of a death at the other extreme of acceptability to hers, that of Colette at the age of 81.

> I would watch her sleeping, and the feeling which governed me was that of gratitude. For thirty years of unclouded happiness she had enabled me to live in an enchanted world, and offered me a picture of such greatness that I despair of being able to bear witness to it, though at least I shall have tried. She did me the favour of going out without suffering, like a sun which sinks, at peace with herself and with all that surrounded her.
> How fortunate to die so, ebbing slowly away, honoured, cherished and secure, able to take a leisurely ceremonious farewell of life. I feel choked by sorrow for the untimely and lonely death of my daughter, Sarah. But I copied out this description of the 'natural death' which ended what someone

has called 'a classically full life', because it was nevertheless reassuring. Nan had said that Sarah 'should have become a grand old lady'. At least such things are possible.

In an earlier book, *Close to Colette*, Goudeket, Colette's last husband tells how, like me, he was impelled to write about the person he loved and mourned. '... I tried every night, in the yellow glow of the lamp, to bring our dead hours back to life. It seemed to me that sometimes another hand guided mine. Those were literally enchanted nights, in a silence that was no longer a loneliness.'

He wrote in a very different mood to mine, and with much greater ease, but this account has given me reassurance, and a sense of fellowship. I too, despite the repeated assaults of doubt about myself as a writer, despite the pain of recalling what was so abruptly destroyed, have discovered the deep satisfaction of recording past happiness.

And I identify with another passage from *Close to Colette*. Goudeket tells of his return to Paris after the First World War, to the life of a well-off thirty-year-old bachelor, besieged by matchmakers but obstinately evading commitment to marriage and family. Then he met Colette.

What I felt was the emotion of a man suddenly brought face to face with his destiny, who knows it, and who feels himself called upon to carry it through... My stubborn refusal to engage myself

and my long waiting were now to show that they
had a meaning, or that they were a failure.

The years of living with Sarah, and the task of continuing to serve her beyond death by writing a book worthy of her, are my own confrontation with destiny. The meeting with her, too, was preceded by a long period of non-commitment, years of reading and learning fuelled by a generalised ambition without engagement in any precise task. Some intense and less-intense love affairs too, but no commitment until I became pregnant. Those years were a training on which I now draw, while the lack of established career and institutional ties has left me free for writing about her. So I echo Goudeket: 'My stubborn refusal to engage myself and my long waiting now show that they have a meaning.'

A scrawled pencil note tucked among the typed diary pages: 'For return from Devon – discovery in London Library of the formula I have been looking for – "her life restored, nothing lost."'

I had taken Daniel to Devon for half-term and we had walked in valleys thick with foxglove and played on wide sandy beaches. I don't remember the source of these words, but they held out a promise that my aim in writing about her could be fulfilled – to resurrect her radiant self with such completeness and truth that others would be changed as I had been. I accepted this optimistic promise for years, only slowly coming to understand that neither my memoir nor anyone else's, not even a work of consummate art, could restore a life with 'nothing lost', or do more at best than conjure up fragments of illusion.

A summer dinner with friends, the doors open onto the flowery garden, glad to be together. Then I think of how Sarah would have bubbled with pleasure, how she would have added gaiety. Undiminished (it seems) pain of longing and outrage for her. But now it simply doesn't last. When they have gone and I sit reading in bed, anguish is dulled by drowsiness, comfort and distraction.

A lesson I get nearer to learning: that mourning and memory cease to be a way of staying close to her, and become estranging, sterile, distorting, soporific. Boring even for me. It is not possible to remain near her, only to feel occasional vivid flashes of nearness. Living without her is the only way of living for me now.

What idiocy! Who thinks otherwise? Who is going to be surprised at that?

A hot morning. As I drive down Westbourne Terrace with a holiday shopping list, the empty streets vibrate in the sun, conjuring up past summers in Australia and Italy. Anguished protest that Sarah will never... Lightning review of familiar arguments – uselessness, irreversibility, must learn acceptance… And suddenly I think that is all totally absurd. How can one accept the death of a five-year-old daughter so that one calmly inhabits a world without her? Impossible and unnecessary. Acknowledge protest as belonging now in my life, allow it to surge up as fiercely as it will, even welcome it, since it shows that my love for her is alive. Don't bewilder myself trying to squelch it.

Saturday, my day-off from duties of household and child, from probing and recording. I use it to follow up a clue from Franz Philipp's book about Arthur Boyd:

> Piero di Cosimo's *Death of Procris* was one of Boyd's favourite Florentine paintings in the National Gallery. He has told me so quite often. Theme and mood of the picture – whatever its exact meaning may be – is that of a gentle threne; the animal and half-animal mourners – dog and faun – crouching, inward-inclined, from the horizontal body of the dead girl… the intense watching pose of the seated dog.

I didn't remember the picture, but the dead girl and the watching dog held out a mysterious promise, which Arthur's interest in the picture intensified. I set off for the National Gallery with the urgency that has often sent me chasing after hints from reading – usually about lives or books, this time about a picture. What is it I am looking for? Whatever it is, I don't ever quite find it. I come away slightly disappointed, though without feeling that I have totally wasted my time. Somewhere I have noted down the obvious interpretation that on these quests I hope to find Sarah alive, or to discover the secret of restoring her. But as I walked down the steps of the National Gallery after looking at the *Death of Procris*, I reflected that, on the contrary (or also), I had been hoping for an experience in which the whole force of grief for an untimely death was held in suspension, as sometimes a child's remark can distil the whole of my wonder at inventive, courageous childhood. I don't often find this concentration. I suppose it requires some rare coincidence of an artist's invention with my personal history and need. As two lines of Wordsworth evoke for me the miraculous reality of her existence:

When she I loved looked every day
Fresh as a rose in June.

I didn't find this magical intensity today in the Piero di Cosimo. It held a gentle melancholy, but no hint of the joyful vitality which was ended by death, nor of the suddenness of the change, nor the despair which is fiercer than melancholy.

I used to puzzle over what was meant by a phrase often encountered in biographies following the report of a child's death: 'She never fully recovered.' At the moment it seems simple and obvious – 'She never regained the wish or the ability to take up her life again fully and vigorously; she remained withdrawn from effort and involvement, endlessly convalescing.' Until I had myself experienced, even though intermittently, such an aversion from living in a world in which she had died, I couldn't have understood this.

And perhaps the biographers don't either. Perhaps 'She never fully recovered' is a way of acknowledging that the death of a child has lasting and doleful consequences which they didn't examine closely, and didn't want to.

'How futile it is to try to discover an appropriate response to either a single death or a hundred and thirty-five thousand.' This sentence leaped out at me from a book review by Susan Lardner in *The New Yorker*. It seemed to announce a profound truth, though I copied it out without comment. I must have seen it as an acknowledgment of the complex immensity of response to a deeply-felt encounter with death. So many thoughts and emotions, often contradictory – and yet inadequate, either singly or all together.

In the end, what changes my view of the world and her place in it is simply the fact. Today, the anniversary of her death, I no longer want to think about what she might have become. I can't even imagine her alive beyond that date. She is that far-off child who lived for only five years. Her mystery dries up.

V

New Ventures
1970-1983

About this time I heard from two close friends of student days, who asked what I was 'doing' these days. The question, I knew, referred to professional work. I replied to each of them that I was still so devastated by Sarah's death that I was incapable of doing anything. Not an entirely truthful answer – I had been working on the Sarah book, accumulating notes about her life, and reading and thinking about the various ways in which children's lives have been written about, but that work wasn't yet at a stage where I felt it could be acknowledged. And I didn't concentrate on it with determination, from doubts and uncertainties of all kinds but I think also from a sort of invalidism, a conception of myself as too badly wounded for disciplined effort.

As soon as I had posted my replies, I asked myself whether what I had said was true. Was I still so dominated by the fact of her death that I couldn't give my full attention to anything else? I decided that it was not true, and abandoned my private self-dramatisation as someone incapacitated by grief.

Soon afterwards I took on a large task, though not a 'doing' in the sense my academic friends meant, by buying the freehold of the house in which we had lived for the past fifteen years, a handsome double-fronted early-Victorian house in Holland Park with a large garden, at the back of which was a studio for Erwin. (The escalation of house prices had barely begun. Only a multi-millionaire could afford to buy such a house now.) In the twenties the house had been divided into flats, several of which had been more recently let off as separate rooms, and the whole place was shabby and run-down. I found myself embarked on an ambitious programme of redevelopment. I say 'I', though Erwin and I bought it together and he shared the work of planning and organising, especially in its early stages, but the decision was chiefly mine and so was the brunt of the responsibility.

It was a rash undertaking for total amateurs. I didn't even understand that the rate of interest on the large sum borrowed from the bank could go up, which it did, astronomically. There were disasters with architects, builders and planning authorities, largely due to our ignorance. Property prices were already booming when we began, and we thought that we would recoup our outgoings by selling the redesigned and renovated flats, and get a cheap flat for ourselves, but just before the work was completed, the property market crashed and it seemed for a while that we would have to sell our own flat too. My inheritance from my mother was paid out just then and went straight towards liquidating the bank loan. All this was a not-quite-full-time job for five years, and certainly a re-engagement with the world. In the end we kept our flat and I lived there for the next thirty years.

Before our imprudence became obvious, I bought a small house on the north coast of Majorca. We had been going there *regularly with Daniel on holiday, and had come to love it. Daniel was getting old enough not to need our constant presence, and I did not want him to grow up without getting to know intimately some piece of country, but it was a stroke of immense luck to find the house at Alconasser – overlooking the sea, on a hillside terraced for olives, carobs and lemons, with the mountains behind. The scent of pines in the sun and the presence of the everchanging sea recall the summers of my childhood at Portsea, on Port Phillip Bay, where we also lived for some of the happiest months of Sarah's life. We spent every school holiday thereafter in the Majorcan house, and when Daniel left school and Erwin began to stay for most of the time in Australia I lived there for part of every winter.*

A third new venture into the world was to attend writing classes at the City Lit, first 'Autobiographical Writing', given by Margaret Rose, and then, for several enjoyable years, Naomi Lewis's 'Writing for Pleasure'. I owe each of them an immense debt. Neither exactly taught writing. They provided opportunity, encouragement and an audience, and I discovered that I could write more deftly and on a wider variety of subjects than I had imagined.

Naomi's class was unique. She would talk rapidly for ten minutes or so on some literary topic, either to satisfy the need to talk of someone living alone, or to get us into the right frame of mind, after which she would 'allot some subjects' – three or four new titles added to those carried over from the previous week. With no time for hesitation, we chose a subject and started to scribble. I don't know how long we were given; I never looked at my watch, but somehow, to my own surprise, I always managed to produce a shapely little piece, usually in prose but sometimes in doggerel verse, before the signal to stop was given. Part of the secret was certainly that there was no time to dither. I came to recognise the wispy annunciation of an idea and set to work on it immediately. Perhaps the most important thing I learned from Naomi's class was confidence in distinguishing the shadowy emergence of something that I had something to say about. When time was up, each of us read out our piece. Our abilities varied, but Naomi listened intently to everything, seldom making technical suggestions for improvement but always finding something encouraging to say, without ever seeming to patronise.

The Sarah book was still an untidy collection of detached notes which I didn't know how to transform into a book. I didn't find out from my City Lit classes either, though I once asked Margaret Rose about engaging the help of a private tutor, an idea which would not have worked (one of my University teachers had called me 'contra-suggestible') and which I soon dropped. (Today's consultancies offering 'mentorship' to novice writers had not yet begun to proliferate.) But in a modest way I learned something of the feel of writing effectively. It was a further emergence from the isolation of grief. I also made two close friends, Naomi herself and a fellow student, Annie Bloch, both of whom gave me their affection and support throughout the following years. They became the first to read anything I had written about Sarah, and to encourage me.

I continued to work intermittently on the book, to puzzle over the outrage of her death, to read widely, to collect texts that spoke to me, and to make entries in the Diary of Grief.

I have a feeling of security and richness when I work on this task of preservation, the book about her. It is that state of rejoicing that she was, which is so hard to attain and so often obscured by despair that she is not.

Her death is not the worst that could have happened, for her or for us. For her: out of countless tragically-fated children, I think most often of the three-year-old I read about a few weeks after her death, who died of malnutrition, beating and cigarette burns without ever having known love or physical well-being. For us: having a grossly handicapped child? I read today a comment by the mother of one such child:

> It would be more merciful for the parents to be told the child was dead and never thought of – forgot… Sure, what if you're heartbroken for a while, it's going to wear away, you know? That never wears away. Whether I send him away or keep him at home, it's going to be heartbreak either way, isn't it?

And if Sarah had been rescued by the doctors from asphyxia, but with her intelligence and evident joy in life destroyed by the temporary lack of oxygen? Comparisons which cannot be made, although we do make them. But morally impossible and experientially also, since we each know only our own sorrow.

NEW VENTURES

It's not to my own childhood I will return in my dotage, but to hers. My lost paradise is the one I shared with her. This morning, half asleep, I remembered walking with her in the gardens of Como, the grand colonial mansion on a bluff above the river Yarra, which was the first property acquired by the National Trust of Victoria. It had been raining and the air was warm and still. In the late morning we were almost the only visitors – the news of President Kennedy's assassination had just been announced. But my memory is of immense happiness at being there with her in the stillness, under the cedar trees, in my second childhood, now left far behind, but the one I will remember if ever I reach a third.

Today I threw out a bottle from Braithwaite's Pharmacy in Hawthorn labelled 'Miss Fabian', which had survived previous clean-ups. But I looked at the spare buttons for her rose-coloured velvet party dress, and put them back into the pocket in my work basket, where I hope they will remain for the rest of my life.

'She was the most beautiful and vital little girl I have ever seen, and I've known a good many,' Mrs Hockey said. I cherish her remark, like some rare object I can take out and look at again and again, an objective confirmation of my own belief.

I felt particularly cheerful this morning. The bank manager had been very affable when I saw him to discuss a loan for the work to our house; I had booked our plane seats for the trip home [I was planning to take Daniel to Australia to visit my father], and a brilliant autumn sun was shining as I turned into the park. Then I noticed my own cheerfulness and wondered again how I could feel happy in that life of which she was bereft. It seems like a puzzle to which there is a solution somewhere, and I want to rack my brains to find it.

But by now I think I know what is to be said – nothing much – and yet its no use repeating, 'Yes, she's dead, but life goes on and one must live.' Though there is very little to be *said* about early death, it has to be meditated and felt. Time and feeling must be given to it, though there is no way of describing most of what goes on in that time. Recognise that it is the inexpressible. And reach for the poetic phrase. Just now I felt an impulse to add, after 'Yes, she's dead', 'Queens have died young and fair,' or 'The life of man is as grass'.

From the moment I first decided to write about Sarah, I knew that I must show her through the accumulated detail of her life, remembered as exactly and vividly as I could manage, rather than through the sort of pious eulogistic summary in which the lost one appears unconvincingly perfect. But I have discovered that for her earliest years I have very few specific memories. What at first I took to be memories of her have turned out to be memories of my own joy in watching her. I regret that I did not act on the impulse I felt in my first astonishment at her inventiveness, when she was only two days old, to keep a diary.

But I don't regret it much. It would have been impossible, as I realise on reading *Three Babies,* diaries written by three mothers of young babies at the request of an academic psychologist, Joseph Church. He had planned to collect a large number of such records, but most of his original participants found the assignment impossible to fulfil. Some of them 'contributed valuable fragmentary accounts', but the three published diaries were the only ones to cover the entire first two years, and then in diversely episodic fashion. I couldn't have kept it up either. Too much happened, and I was too involved in its happening. When life is going well one does not need to write about it.

Reading *Three Babies* revives emotions of those first months, when I was an enthralled spectator of Sarah's investigations and discoveries. I feel excited, proud and hopeful, as I did then. I read of baby Ruth turning a photograph round to see the other side and being puzzled that the people have no other side. It gives me a sense of revelation, as if I were witnessing the esssential genius of the human race. And Debbie's bedtime at 2 years 3 weeks:

Wants a kiss, sometimes orders us to kiss a doll in the buggy, and settles down. Door closed, lights off at 7 to 7.30 and Debbie is usually entirely quiet immediately, although once in a great while she may jabber a bit to her bedmates about some of the day's problems. (e.g. 'Baby! Eat! No? All done?

OK.' or 'Help bear? Go potty. Do wee-wee, OK?' 'OK. All done. Get down. Help bear?') for five or ten minutes.

Immensely touching. Not because I laugh or feel superior. Admiration and thankfulness, a breathless sense of being in the presence of grace, a feeling that is the counter-part to terror and awe before something immense and inexplicable. But I don't want to suggest God-given. Inexplicable means not deserved. Not undeserved either.

But another explanation of why writing a satisfying infant diary is impossible: they rapidly become boring. I am moved by *Three Babies* only if I read it in small doses, and then not by every entry. And, like earlier parental diaries from Darwin on, they seem to miss much of whatever it is that now, looking back, I most urgently want to grasp and express.

I will fail in writing about her, too. So why do I plug on? Out of love and loyalty to her, and a shadowy belief that it will please her. From a need to bear witness. And because I recognise in her a 'sacred being' – a concept defined by W. H. Auden, in an essay which has helped me to understand what I am doing, and sustained my belief in its rightness. I have copied out large chunks of his essay, and reread them often.

> The impression made upon the imagination by any sacred being is of an overwhelming but undefinable importance – an unchangeable quality, an identity, as Keats said: I-am-that-I-am is what every sacred being seems to say... The impulse to create a work

> of art is felt when, in certain persons, the passive awe provoked by sacred beings or events is transformed into a desire to express that awe in a rite of worship or homage…

Sarah was a sacred being for me from the moment she was born; I experienced that overwhelming recognition of identity, and responded with joyous wonder, which her death transformed into the need to make an act of homage. And perhaps my attempt to convey something of her miraculous essence will not totally fail.

Margaret said that she doesn't know how I survived Sarah's death – a comment no-one else has made. I am grateful for this recognition of how intense the struggle has been and is; it helps me to feel I still live in the same world as other people.

A piece I wrote for Margaret Rose's class at the City Lit. She asked us for a 'diary entry'. My initial reaction was that I couldn't possibly write a genuine diary entry which would be of interest in isolation. It never occurred to me to write a fictional one, as some of the others did. In the end, I wrote a piece that was both truthful and self-contained, and felt quite pleased with it.

> After studying the reproductions in Picasso's World of Children, I have been trying to formulate what he says about children in these pictures. Nothing very much. I don't mean 'nothing very important',

but nothing that would fill up many lines of writing. Most of the pictures are completely non-anecdotal. A child sits in a chair looking straight ahead – that doesn't tell us much about children.

But then I go on looking at the child's face. It seems to convey something about his character, or mood, or outlook on the world, but what? I can draw up a list of adjectives – calm, confident, waiting, expectant, admiring ... perhaps also a little apprehensive. I could go on adding to the list, but already it begins to lose resonance.

And then suddenly I see (perhaps not a new idea even for me, but for a moment I understand it more clearly than before) that what Picasso is saying about children, what a painter can say about anything, is different from what a writer can say. More concentrated, more intense, more elusive – and different. So we aren't competing, Picasso and I. I can go on trying to write about children without feeling that one of the great geniuses of our time has already said it all.

The book reproduces pictures of Picasso's four children, each series different in style and content. His first-born son Paulo is always calm, still, and handsome. In the latest painting, *Paulo as Torero*, he looks astonishingly beautiful, with a grave reflective face that is ageless. I can accept that he is only four, but he could almost be eighteen. Paulo is man not yet wounded and scarred by the world.

NEW VENTURES

Days recently that have felt like days of recovery. Of acceptance that my life must go on without her – new enthusiasms, new vigour, new projects with which she has little or nothing to do. But acceptance also that her death doesn't disappear, and can't be incorporated into this continuing life. To contemplate her death is to see everything collapse and lose meaning, to have no desires. That will recur. I want it to recur. There isn't any way of understanding and accepting her death that fits it into a personal life stretching into the future. To acknowledge her death means to accept two modes of existence.

A death is not an event that occurs on a particular day and then is over, left behind in the past. It is a continuing, dominating presence. A revelation of the years since her death and a discovery that has transformed my perception of the lives of other survivors.

I have never been comforted by the thought that the physical body survives by becoming part of other living creatures. But the spirit also is reincorporated into life – her spirit, her courageous joyful self. Into me, through these years of loving and thinking about her; into Erwin and Daniel through their memories; eventually perhaps into persons unknown to me, through what I write about her.

Parents who receive messages from their dead children through poltergeistish signs – scents, music and laughter, or displaced books and postcards arranged in peculiar patterns; parents who visit mediums and receive explicit messages from the dead; Rosamund Lehmann and Bishop Jim Pike, both of whose books I have read several times, without accepting their beliefs, but also without the scorn I would once have felt. Instead, I sympathise with grief so wounding that it breeds bizarre convictions and involvements. And sometimes, in a wispy fleeting way I share their fantasies, Rosamund Lehmann's especially. I don't accept her evidence of survival, but I share her longings, and sometimes I am glad that *she* believes.

Bishop Pike tells stories about mediums who showed a familiarity with facts of his past life which they 'could not possibly have known'. I have wondered why I feel no impulse to investigate such stories more closely. But my fundamental unbelief is far too strong for me to contemplate spending the time and effort. And the Bishop presents his case with a mixture of logical reasoning and dubious assumption that does not inspire confidence. And then if there were that much to it, someone else would have done some respectable research before now – and no doubt has.

Twenty-five years later, Bishop Pike has slipped back into obscurity. The Kensington librarian has never heard of him.

NEW VENTURES

Naomi Lewis last Thursday read out a comment that a character in a story by Eudora Welty 'hadn't a sense of her own tragedy'. There was a discussion about whether it was a good thing for a writer to have a sense of his own tragedy. Naomi said she thought it important to do something about tragedy, rather than simply to lament it. Someone else said that to be aware of one's own tragedy, to talk about it, was a self-indulgent luxury, and everyone seemed to approve of this. I disagreed, but silently, not wanting to reveal my personal involvement in the question. But isn't a writer's contribution to make people more aware, not by doing but by expressing? And what do most of us write out of if not our own tragedy?

The common accusation of self-pity often haunts me. My private defence is that self-pity is passive – a hopeless bewailing to oneself and others. My preoccupation with grief is active and at least sometimes detached – a continuous study of myself, true, but also reading, comparing, searching. Not self-pity but self-observation, self-education and perhaps self-transformation.

And sometimes I think, 'Why not self-pity?' If I do not pity myself, who will pity me? And then – I don't want other people's pity, my own is enough.

I don't often make entries in the Diary of Grief now, because the themes of grief have become familiar and I have written about most of them. And because I see more clearly that the essence of grief is a turning away from the world and everything in it, including thought, psychological observation and the effort to find words to describe states of being. An engulfment in sorrow, longing, appalment and terror, which can't be conveyed by writing.

And then a totally different reason: having written two 'diary entries' for the writing class, I see how much work must go into them before they convey my meaning in a moving and communicable way. At present I feel a distaste for working intensively on my diary entries, but I suspect that my scrappy notes won't inspire me to do so in the future. The essence of a diary is to capture feelings of the moment and how can you do that except at the moment?

So having explained why I am ceasing to write DG notes, here is one: I have just read in an article on Delacroix by V.S. Pritchett: 'The great Journals are written by solitaries and are obsessional.' With faulty logic, I draw encouragement for this diary from Pritchett's remark. Solitary and obsessive I no doubt am, and defensive about it. I have told a number of people that I am writing about Sarah, but not a soul about this diary, not even Erwin, because it is about my own feelings and reactions, and I expect to be condemned or pitied. Self-absorption is another cardinal sin these days. But it doesn't feel like self-absorption. It feels like an encounter with a massive, ancient, powerful reality, about which I continually make new discoveries.

I have added to my hoard of texts several from a poet new to me, Dame Mary Gilmore.

> Nurse no long grief
> Lest the heart flower no more.
> Grief builds no barns; its crops
> Rot at the door.

Patently false – grief builds many barns, some ramshackle, others strong and beautiful as wooden cathedrals. But it is a common sentiment, so it is with irony that I repeat, 'Grief builds no barns!' (Mild irony I suppose, tempered with dubious assent.)

From Mary Gilmore also:

> All men shall sit at God's right hand,
> And all men shall be fed;
> But this bread in my hand,
> This is my son's bread.

This became, over the years, one of my essential incantations, which I repeated whenever I felt a stab of shame at being so preoccupied with Sarah's one natural death in a world everywhere darkened by the slaughter of the innocent.

Lighting a fire in the late afternoon to warm a house which had become gloomy and cold as the Majorcan winter sun declined, something I have not done since Sarah was alive, when we used to light the fire in the Power Street sitting room before beginning the reading lessons which were one of the pleasures of her last months. They were surrounded by ritual. First she insisted on carrying a heavy mallee root in from the woodshed in the garden. The fire was already laid. I lit a match and she applied it cautiously to the paper. As the flames sprang up, we sat back on the red chintz sofa, and she chose a 'pointer' from a selection of bent paper-clips, knitting needles, and plastic modelling tools. Then we continued our rapid progress through the excellent series of word books which I had found in an educational bookshop, hidden on a lower shelf below a display of the modish 'Look and Say' method. Our reading lessons were a source of pride and pleasure for both of us. And she was learning rapidly. We progressed in a few days from boot and book to candle and bubble.

This morning the man at the Soller garage asked Daniel to hold the petrol hose while he pumped, because the electric motor had broken down. He was surprised that Daniel didn't understand. 'I thought he was Mayorquin,' he said, and then, disbelievingly, 'He is not your son?' I nodded and laughed, asking did he think I was too old, with my grey hair. 'Only the one?' I nodded again. He looked sad. I said, 'I had a daughter but she died at five.' Before I had finished, he understood, and his unshaven face took on a look of concern. He said, 'These things happen in life.' And then told me that he himself has only one son, although he has been married ten years. 'Ten years!' he repeated. The natural spontaneous sympathy of this man, touched me deeply. It is a response I have often wanted in vain. I had begun to think that I was asking for something totally unreasonable and impossible.

We never spoke again of these matters, but I always felt,

whenever I saw him, that there was a special bond of understanding between us.

On our way home after the Easter holiday, we stayed in France for an extra day to celebrate her birthday by visiting a new place – Villequier, on the Seine estuary, where Victor Hugo used to stay with his son-in-law's family. Their house now holds a collection of Hugo mementos: autograph letters, portraits, the carved four-poster bed in which he slept, a model of Notre Dame with a clock in its facade presented by his publisher, a model of his catafalque made from human hair. I looked out from the upstairs windows across a garden bright with tulips and wallflowers to the wide river, while Daniel watched the ships move upstream towards Rouen. It was a vivid and enjoyable day to add to previous anniversaries in beautiful places. But the festive associations accumulate because I want to make the day of her birth a day of rejoicing, not because thanksgiving spontaneously overflows into celebration. And by now the celebration is my own private affair. I stopped trying to mark her birthday by some shared festivity, after a dinner when Cecily failed to recognise the date, and another which Erwin sabotaged in a mood of hostility. An attempt to establish a ritual has completely flopped.

But since he began to live most of the time in Australia, Erwin always telephones me on her birthday and on her deathday.

I leave this piece as I wrote it, but it now seems extraordinary that I did not mention that Hugo's daughter

Cécile was drowned in that wide river. I blotted this bereavement from my remembrance of the day, but soon afterwards I added Hugo, unfavourably, to my gallery of archetypes, after reading several of the poems he wrote about Cécile's death. They combine enormous egotism and appalling vapidity.

> Je verrai cet instant jusqu'à ce que je meure,
> L'instant, pleurs superflus!
> Où je criai: L'enfant que j'avais tout à l'heure,
> Quoi donc! je ne l'ai plus!

I shall see that moment until my dying day, the moment when, beyond tears, I cried: The child who just now was mine , well, she is mine no longer!

'The greatest of French poets – Victor Hugo, hélas!' Hélas indeed!

A few days ago I found myself saying casually to a comparative stranger, in the course of conversation, 'I had a daughter who died, and when the children were small…' I reflected afterwards that this was a milestone, a measure of the detachment I have achieved. But yesterday I received a letter from the Probate Personal Application Department, which I have at last contacted in order to collect and transfer to Daniel Sarah's small estate – £160 in savings certificates bought with money my mother gave me for her. The official letter stirred up rage, protest and the sense of being close to tears, and does again now, as I re-read it.

Will you please attend at Room 111 (first floor) at the above address on Tuesday 4th March 1975 at

11.30 am and hand this letter to the clerk or messenger in attendance as soon as you arrive. If you are unable to keep this appointment, will you please write here or telephone 01 836 7366, when you will be given another appointment.

Should it be difficult for you to make this first visit, a close relative or friend who is personally aware of the facts may attend on your behalf, but it will be necessary for you to attend personally on a later occasion.

I don't like any of that. Especially not the phrase 'should it be difficult for you to make this first visit'. Obviously, you clots, it is difficult for me. And also none of your business. And then the note at the bottom, 'In all communications to the Department, the name of the deceased and reference number should be quoted, and the date of your appointment.' It stops me from ringing up to change the appointment, which happens to clash with my annual visit to the Royal Marsden. I don't want to have to say her name to them, or to reveal any corner of my private grief. And I rage still at the explanation, obviously intended to make the occasion less formidable, that it may be necessary to wait: 'Wait? My God they owe me the consideration of making sure I don't have to wait. And then why all this cumbrous fuss? Just to show how important they are?' And so on. It's impossible to say the right thing to the bereaved, who, moreover, will misinterpret your innocent words to give them a hurtful meaning.

I thought the date of this entry must be wrong. I could hardly believe I had still been so touchy ten years after her death, nor that I had waited so long to attend to this small bureacratic duty. But the original note is clearly dated 12 February 1975.

Two quotations from Spanish poets have been haunting me. From Antonio Machado:
  Mi corazón està donde ha nacido
  no a la vida, al amor, cerca del Duero.
  My heart lies where it was born, not to life, but to love, near the Duero.

I repeat Machado's lines to affirm that everything important in my life began with her. My heart was born, not to life, but to love, with her birth.

The reference to the Duero evokes Machado's poems about the cold city of Soria, encircled by that river, where he met his wife Leonora, and where five years later she died, and about the surrounding bare fields and arid mountains of Castille. And my own sight of Soria and of Moncayo, a mountain which, in homage to Machado, I climbed with Daniel and his friend Ambrose at the end of a school holiday. The heat, aridity and emptiness of Castille recall Australia, country of my own childhood and of the happiest years with Sarah. All of that links me to Machado. When I repeat 'My heart lies where it was born, not to life but to love, by the Duero,' I acknowledge the sacred reality of that upsurge of happiness in midlife, preceded by years of humdrum ordinariness (so it now seems), and followed by desolation, yet the source of continuing joy and strength.

With the same conviction of making an essential discovery, I have seized on a sentence from another Spanish poet, Pedro Salinas, written in what my friend Maria calls 'poet's prose':

Viven en este triste modo de existencia que consiste en saber que fueron, nada màs.

They live in that sad form of existence which consists in the knowledge that they were, nothing more.

The word that resonates for me here is not 'sad', but 'existence.' Salinas was writing about the Spanish national epic, *The Poem of the Cid*, which, he suggests, cannot have been the first Castillian epic poem, since many details of its technique indicate an established tradition. But the words and the very titles of those earlier poems were irrevocably lost when 'the humble parchment on which they were inscribed was torn apart by unknown hands, left to rot in some patch of Castillian soil, and finally scattered as dust in the wind.' Yet Salinas asserts with loving reverence that the simple knowledge that they once were is a form of continuing existence. How much more certainly then must she still exist, whose words and being remain in my memory and in that of many others? And even more if I succeed in publishing a book which will be read by people who did not know her in her lifetime. I repeat to myself: 'Viven en este triste modo de existencia que consiste en saber que fueron, nada màs', defying moralists who urge me to accept that she has utterly vanished from the world.

A beautiful documentary last night about three remote valleys in the Hindu Kush, home of the Kalash, who commemorate their eminent dead with larger-than-life-size wooden effigies. According to the director, Daniel Topolski, most of these have been stolen by 'voracious European dealers [who] braved the wrath of the spirits and the overwhelming smell to desecrate the cemeteries and altars.' But we saw one handsome young man visit the wooden statue of his grandfather, to touch him familiarly on the chest, and bring him up to date with the latest news of family, animals and crops. Enviable, enviable. I wish we had such a custom. I don't think I would need to believe that she heard, but sanctification by society and time would give the performance a weight and seriousness that private make-believe lacks.

I have been writing about Sarah's shoes for SB. The scuffed brown lace-ups I used to push onto her uncooperative feet clearly belong to the story of her life. The plastic sandal she threw out of the car window near Rye back beach, and which perhaps remains there among the marram-grass roots, half-covered with sand, just squeezes in, though it is only since her death that I have imagined it lying there still. But reluctantly, recognising that they belong only to the time of grief, I omit the blue rubber thongs with the imprint of her grubby bare feet, which I found in the woodshed by the back door, weeks after she died.

We cherish finding after a death things still lying where they were left in life, because the vanished life, its ordinary happiness, rapidly comes to seem impossible. These tangible eloquent objects are proof that she did really once exist.

I live without her now. Even writing, most of the time, is no longer something I do for her, but a struggle for my own sake to overcome incapacitating dreads and the intractabilities of language. But sometimes a sight or a word make me suddenly aware of her again, not as an absence but as an existence, and I feel a fleeting return of hope and former joy. It happened yesterday while I was talking to Naomi Lewis about the book. 'You must finish it for her,' she said. I habitually half-believe that she will know and be pleased by the tribute I want to pay her, but I have never dared to share the thought with anyone. Naomi's remark gave me sharp pleasure. Not quite a confirmation, but a strengthening and legitimising of my fantasy.

'All art is murder.' I heard this or something like it, in a lecture on artistic creation by a psychoanalyst. I don't remember when or by whom, and I can't find any reference to it in notes or diaries, but I have thought about it repeatedly and recognise its truth. To write about her I have to look at the facts of her life with a craftsman's appraising eye, ignoring impulses to love and comfort. Soul-murder at least, but unavoidable. I recite Blake's injunction, 'Drive your cart and your plough over the bones of the dead.' I am writing SB to please her, but also committing an atrocity against her.

'Streets filled with other people's daughters' (Rosamund Lehmann's phrase) I accept easily enough most of the time. But there are families whose living flourishing daughters were born close in time to mine, and whom I sometimes envy malevolently. Last night we had dinner with such a father, whom I have known for a very long time, who nursed Sarah when she was a baby. He spoke of his daughter's approach to the time of sexual experimentation, and of his dislike, fear, and powerlessness. 'It's better to have a son – girls are much more vulnerable,' he said, looking at me with no sign of remembering Sarah's existence. And I nodded and didn't say, 'Well it's better to be afraid for a living daughter than to be stuck in longing and outrage for a dead one.'

I was recently at another dinner with a group of old friends. Our children had all been born within a few years of each other. 'Such marvellous children!' they agreed. 'They've had such wonderful childhoods. It will be interesting to see what becomes of them.' No-one gave any sign of recalling what had become of her.

I am both incredulous and impressed when I learn of someone who appears to reject grief. Gavin Young writes in *Return to the Marshes* about Sayyid Sarwat, a patriarch of the Marsh Arabs, now over 80: 'When one of his sons

– a favourite son – was killed in a motor-cycle accident a year or two ago, people commiserated with him. The old man brushed them gently aside, saying "It was written." And another oddly moving incident: Gavin Young's friend Arjam had a first son, Kharaibat, whom he called 'Mister' Kharaibat in honour of Mister Young. 'But Mister Kharaibat died quite soon.' When Young returned to the marshes twenty years later, Arjam asked him, 'Do you remember my first son's birthday party?' 'I remember Mister Kharaibat very well.' I was touched by the remembering, and by his use of the full name, suggesting that the baby son still lived in his mind as an individual.

Paul Fussell writes that Siegfried Sassoon was 'one of those for whom remembering the war became something like a life work.' Ah, I think, if he accepts that for Sassoon, then it is permissible for me also to make remembering *her* my life's work. In a selfish and mad way, or in a sane and generous way? Sometimes I don't know the difference.

I picked up by chance in Dillon's a book which introduced me to a new literary genre, and to a thousand-year-old grief. The newly-discovered genre is the Japanese poetic diary, a form which fuses prose and verse in a way unknown in Western tradition but which has been cultivated in Japan from before the year 1000 up to the present day. The diaries offer a prosaically factual record of daily events (or purport to, since their content is acknowledged by literary historians to be at least in part fictional and shaped by the requirements of art), which is interspersed with poems in the short intense Japanese forms, tanka and haiku. The editor of this collection of poetic diaries, Earl Miner, comments that they 'combine, or poise, two formal energies: the ceaseless pressure of time implied by the diary form itself, and the enhancement of the moment in poetry.'

The earliest example he prints, *The Tosa Diary*, is a contemporary-seeming masterpiece dating from some time between 935 and 1370, which tells of the return journey by sea from Tosa to Kyoto of a provincial governor and his entourage at the end of his term of office. Its ostensible author is a woman, writing in a tone of pervasive melancholy whose cause is only revealed on the seventh day, after she has described the lengthy ceremonies of farewell.

> Amid all these things which I have related, I was filled with grief for my daughter. She had been born in the capital and had died suddenly in the province. Because of all the commotion of our departure, I have said nothing about this, but now that we are at last bound for the capital, I cannot help longing to have my dead girl alive again. The people with me wish her with us, too. I made some verses.
>
> The greatest sadness
> Of thinking that now at last
> We are bound for home

> Is that there remains one person
> Who will never know return.

After that, she frequently writes of her lost child, in prose and in verse, while telling of small incidents on the journey. When the party finally arrived in Kyoto, the diarist found her house in ruins and the garden overgrown.

I composed a poem which I did not tell to the others:
> She was born here,
> And although she did not return,
> When back in this house
> I look upon the little pines grown here
> With grief for one who grows no more.

That ancient grief is identical with mine in essence and in many details, especially in the desolation of returning home after a long absence without the daughter who was born there. The plain language speaks directly to today, and I find a deep and lasting pleasure in this sharing across centuries.

A letter from Thomas Hardy to Rider Haggard:
> Please give my kind regards to Mrs Haggard and tell her how deeply our sympathy was with you both in your bereavement. Though, to be candid, I think the death of a child is never really to be regretted, when one reflects on what he has escaped.

An absurd letter to write to a newly-bereaved parent. The view that its best never to have been born, and next best to die young, is not one that I have ever held, even briefly, and I could not possibly think so about her.

Later I came across a similar letter, from Ernest Hemingway to the golden couple of the twenties, Sara and Gerald Murphy, on the death of their eldest son:

> Absolutely truly and coldly in the head, though, I know that anyone who dies young after a happy childhood, and no one ever made a happier childhood than you made for your children, has won a great victory. We all have to look forward to death by defeat, our bodies gone, our world destroyed; but it is the same dying we must do, while he has gotten it all over with, his world all intact and the death only by accident.

I owe this discovery to Anthony Burgess who thought the letter 'superb.' I think it is heartless and cruel, particularly since the child died not by any sudden accident but after a long and gruelling illness. I prefer Hardy's plainness, but to me, since I am not the desolate parent who received them, both letters are absurd. Unlike Hardy, Hemingway and Burgess were parents, although not bereaved parents.

No newly-bereaved parent of a young child would be convinced or consoled by such an argument. A mother whose daughter had died some years before, at the age of three, once told me, 'At first I was desolate, but I have come to believe that she spread so much happiness around her in those three years that she had done all that she was put on earth to do.' But that is the absolute opposite – not a rejection of life but a celebration.

Two children are playing in the garden, a boy of about four and his younger sister. Their voices, in which intelligence and self-assurance show through the childish intonations, stir up envy and longing. I observe with tenderness their self-contained play together, the boy fetching his sister to join him in filling yogurt cups with earth, their unselfconsciousness, and the rounded beauty of the girl's body as she runs naked on the grass. I long for them to accept and confide in me as freely as they do to each other. But I don't go down to the garden to make their acquaintance. From shyness, busyness with other matters, a sense of having lost the ability to talk easily to children, but also because I know our meeting would be brief. They would be summoned back to their own lives and I would feel abandoned. It has happened before. What I really want is to be their mother.

Some people can immediately enter into the confidence of newly-met children, as Cecily could, or Annie Maxwell; even then, the communion is short-lived – but for the rest of us unattainable.

Helen Thomas, in *World Without End:*
> I lie thinking of the strange bewilderment of things that is our life. I cannot understand it: birth, love, death and all the different kinds of suffering; the loneliness of each one in spite of friendship and love and sympathy; David and me and Margaret ... What can it mean?

David and Margaret were the names Helen Thomas used in writing about her husband, the poet Edward Thomas, and Eleanor Farjeon, Edward's lover, who was also her own friend. Helen Thomas's autobiographical books, *As It Was* and *World Without End,* tell the story of her marriage with moving simplicity and honesty. When I first resolved to write Sarah's life, I took *As It Was* for one of my models.

Curious, that baffled sense of elusive meaning. I don't feel it for those three. Their story includes conflict, complex emotions, the transitoriness of both despair and happiness, difficult situations to ponder, but no intimation of a central hidden 'meaning'. But I have felt it strongly and often about Sarah's death, and about grief for the youthful dead, even while I reject the whole notion of hidden meaning. I track down books because of some small hint, and research the biographies of bereft parents in pursuit of – something. 'Answer' or 'meaning' is too definite.

Egotistically, I feel her death as a belittlement. In the first months there were people I hated having to face in my diminished state – mainly I think those connected with business, with whom my relationship was scarcely personal and status was important. To be the parent of a dead daughter looks like a weak and contemptible state, just as to be the parent of a beautiful, intelligent child is accepted as a cause for pride and self-exaltation. Byron's cruel comment on Mary Shelley that she couldn't even raise a child. Freud saying that he felt his daughter Sophie's death as 'a deep narcissistic wound'. Though I have always been puzzled as to what he meant by adding that his wife and Anna mourned 'in a more human way'. I imagine he simply jibbed at attributing to them also the egotism of that 'narcissistic wound'.

I have kept a cutting from the *Diario de Mallorca* about Trinidad, an eight-year old girl from a village in the rural centre of the island, who failed to come home from school one day; no trace of her was found despite island-wide police searches. Months later, a man out walking with his dog came across the remains of a body and some clothing, including a red woollen scarf, under a bush on a hillside near the village. The child's father was summoned, and recognised the scarf. 'Si,' he said. 'Es mi Trini'. (It is my Trini.) 'Es mi Trini' is a macabre version of the insistence that she still exists – and an inescapably true one.

Delayed by fog in Venice airport, I sat next to a young, unhappy, half-Italian woman travelling alone with her six-month-old baby. She looked very tired and I offered to hold the baby, a beautiful flirtatious girl, who played energetically at pushing with her feet, smiling and relishing praise. Eventually she became fretful, was fed and then changed with a lot of fuss in the VIP lounge, and finally fell asleep in my arms. Great pleasure in her liveliness, in sharing the slow tasks of caring for her, in her weight against my arm and the familiar enduring of a cramped, uncomfortable position so that she could sleep undisturbed. It is the first time since Sarah died that I have held a baby for so long.

I have been reading, in *Seven Years Old*, the Newsons' survey of mothers' attitudes, the answers to a question which they felt got to the 'nub of the relationship'. 'Now that N is seven, what is it about him that gives you most pleasure?'

> Companionship was markedly emphasised by mothers of girls in particular... Often the mother was quite explicit that it was the femininity of her daughter that she found satisfying... And not merely that little girls are nice to dress and 'titivate up'... It is more a question of shared feminine interests and attitudes that have very deep roots.

Working on the last chapters of the Sarah book and living with her again in memory, I don't feel as stabbed by this as I would have earlier. I imagine the talks and outings we could still be having, but I also recall with gratitude that we did share a feminine closeness. 'Are you wearing a sleeveless dress today?' she would ask. Sleevelessness was the fashion just then and it extended even to dresses for little girls. If I said yes, she wanted to wear one too.

Some time ago, I copied out a passage from the Oxford philosopher Rush Rhees, which was quoted in a review of his book *Without Answers*:

> Suppose there has been an earthquake and geologists now give an explanation of it. This will not be an answer to the woman who has lost her home and her child and asks 'Why?' It does not make it easier to understand 'what has befallen us'. And the woman's question, though it may drive her mad, does not seek an answer.

What did Rhees mean by saying she did not seek an answer? And if not an answer, what was she seeking? I don't think I ever asked, 'Why, why me, why her?' I knew there were no answers to those questions, but I seemed to have been trying to find an answer to some question which I hadn't clearly formulated. I felt a spurt of hope that Rhees's book might enable me to understand what her questions, and perhaps mine, were seeking if not 'answers', and I looked for a copy. It was not an easy book to find and I had to wait for it to be produced through the Inter-Library Loan system. When at last it arrived, it was no help. Rhees added nothing to the words quoted in the review and, reading further, I found that he habitually made bold assertions without adding anything in the way of elaboration, argument or defence, simply planting them down and moving on to the next point. So I must just accept that there are states of puzzlement to which there is no answer, and which don't really demand an answer.

A visit to Dr Adler, the eccentric, garrulous, dedicated general practitioner and friend, who delivered both Sarah and Daniel, and to whom I owe my life for his prompt management of an emergency after Daniel was born. He spoke of two of his friends who had fatal heart attacks very soon after being discharged from hospital, outrageously in his opinion. His judgment of doctors and of hospitals can be scathing. He went on, 'Your daughter who died in Australia – that was a matter of wrong diagnosis.' I don't remember anyone using just that particular blunt phrase before, and I thought, 'Now at last I understand!' accompanied by a vivid flash of belief that now we could return and do it right. Then renewed anguish because that opportunity, if there had ever been one, had gone forever. I surprise myself by this reaction. How persistent hope is, despite the absolute knowledge that there is no hope! It endures because of the fierceness of longing; it is longing that is unquenchable.

Now, 1993, I don't feel that Dr Adler made anything clearer. His remark only makes me angry at his presumptuous omniscience and obtuse stirring-up of painful feelings. I have remembered for years, with pain and resentment, similar pronouncements by friends: 'Bad doctoring', 'I don't understand how she could have died.' No-one should ever say such things, not with that dismissive knowingness.

From an article about The Compassionate Friends, the self-help association for bereaved parents: 'The readjustment is solitary because the bereaved are often avoided or met with silence on the subject of their dead child, when their greatest need is to talk.' Well yes, a bit of talk does help. But grief is also solitary because grieving is too repetitious and boring for anyone to share for long. And also because it is the immensity and uniqueness of her life that I mourn. Not even another bereaved parent can know that. No-one except Erwin can share the intensity of feeling I still have for her.

At some moment, I don't remember quite when, I discovered the word 'fulminating': 'developing suddenly or rapidly; a fulminating disease'. It seemed to explain the mystery of why an ordinary chest infection could kill her. 'She died of a fulminating disease.' For a while, I seemed to understand.

Do I think there is any possibility that Sarah might still live somewhere, as Rosamund Lehmann believes her daughter does? No, I don't. But now, when the possibility occurs to me, I no longer feel such a necessity to push it sternly away. I don't at all believe, but I think I have earned the indulgence of pretence, of imagining. Only very briefly – it's not a fantasy I am tempted to embroider, not as strong as 'hoping it might be so', but a faint shadow of that hope must be, for me, part of what makes Hardy's poem 'The Oxen' so moving.

Christmas Eve, and twelve of the clock.
'Now they are all on their knees,'
An elder said as we sat in a flock
By the embers in hearthside ease.

We pictured the meek mild creatures where

> They dwelt in their strawy pen.
> Nor did it occur to one of us there
> To doubt they were kneeling then.
>
> So fair a fancy few believe
> In these years! Yet, I feel,
> If someone said on Christmas Eve
> 'Come; see the oxen kneel
>
> 'In the lonely barton by yonder comb
> Our childhood used to know,'
> I should go with him in the gloom,
> Hoping it might be so.

It is only since she died that I have got to know Hardy's poetry, and in particular the poems of remembrance for his dead wife. They don't all speak of her – I have not had to master the bitterness of acknowledging misunderstanding and neglect. But many of Hardy's backward-looking moods express my feelings about her, especially his variations on the theme of places which bear eternally the mark of a fleeting presence:

> Primaeval rocks form the road's steep border,
> And much have they faced there, first and last,
> Of the transitory in Earth's long order;
> But what they record in colour and cast
> Is – that we two passed.

Sometimes the memory flashes into mind of a place where we were together, a scene that appears to carry a message of transcendent significance. I wanted to describe every one of these occasions in the book about Sarah. But then I realised that they are numinous only for me, and that it takes a poet of the stature of Hardy to convey the strength and preciousness of this sense of past happiness permanently imprinted on a landscape. So I reconcile myself to cherishing my memories in private, and instead reread 'At Castle Boterel', or 'Green Slates', or 'Where the Picnic Was'.

Typing the last chapters of the finished draft of SB, especially the one on bedtimes, when we were very close and she showed her need for my protectiveness, I feel happy and calm and blessed. As if she is still present in a timeless world. And isn't that what I have been trying to achieve? The possibility described by Pasternak, in a lost lecture which he summarised for Olga Andreyev Carlisle: 'Although the artist will die, the happiness of living which he has experienced is immortal. If it is captured in a personal and yet universal form it can actually be relived by others through his work.' By others perhaps – but certainly by oneself.

There is consolation in having 'done something' with her death. And at the moment I do feel that I have done something in finishing the book, irrespective of whether or not it is ever published. I am better pleased with myself than for a long time.

VI

Something Done
1983 – 1988

Eighteen years after Sarah died, I completed a draft of the book about her, which I called 'A Shining Space'. Freshly typed, it had a convincing air of completeness and finality. I asked a number of friends to read it, expecting to be damned with faint and embarrassed praise, but met instead with enough convincing appreciation to give my confidence a needed boost. I also sent it to a succession of literary agents and publishers. No-one was prepared either to represent me or to publish it, but contrary to received folk-wisdom, I seldom got it back without a detailed letter which showed that it had been thoughtfully considered. The realities of packing-up the typescript, sending it off, imagining it physically present in someone's office, even receiving it back with a negative verdict, all felt bracingly actual after those long years of secrecy precariously sustained by fantasies of triumphant success.

In the light of the comments I received, I looked at the book from new perspectives. An experienced editor, now retired, to whom a mutual friend had introduced me, wrote, 'It is not publishable as it stands.' Her verdict was a salutary shock. I did not accept all her reasons, but I saw for myself, on rereading, that the book was often ragged in structure and unresonant in content. I would have to rethink, reorganise and rewrite. Soon what lay on my desk had changed from a book into a dismembered corpse awaiting resurrection, but I was now confident of my ability to produce a new and better version.

Meanwhile I had begun to mull over the problems of making a readable edited version of the Diary of Grief. When I sorted its scattered pages, the earliest I could find were dated about a year after Sarah's death. I couldn't remember when I had begun to separate observations about grief from other diary writings, and wondered if there might be some earlier pages, stashed away with other notes in dusty brown envelopes in the loft or on top of the wardrobe. I didn't find anything labelled DG, but I did find a packet entitled 'Daniel and Sarah', which turned out to be a record of Daniel's reactions to his beloved sister's death – his questions, comments, moods and eloquent games. He was not quite three when she died. I had totally forgotten ever having kept such a diary, and I found it moving and uplifting. It revealed in a very young child human strengths of courage, truthfulness and imagination as unexpected and admirable as those which shone through my memories of Sarah's life, and which I had wanted to preserve by writing about her.

I thought 'something could be done' with this discovery. I put the ragged swatch of notes into chronological order and started to type them. As I did so, I saw that not much had to be 'done'. The diary already told its own story. I need only tidy it up a bit, cut out some repetition and write an introduction and some pieces of connecting narrative to turn it into the book which was eventually published as The Daniel Diary. *By comparison with my other two books, the one about Sarah and this Diary of Grief, its birth was painless.*

My own life at this time also needed reordering. Daniel had finished school and was wandering the world. Erwin was living most of the time in Melbourne. I was left alone in the London flat. I have always been something of a solitary but I had not bargained for this much solitude, and there were stressful times before I learned to accept and make use of it. I have thought of that period as another bereavement, but it was very different from the mourning for Sarah. The emotions I wrestled with centred only on myself and, although they were painful, I never pretended that a new tragedy had befallen me. The two who had left me were responsible for their own lives. And they were not, after all, dead. There was nothing to parallel my appalled, baffled, desperate, endless involvement with her fate and what it meant for her.

I put the problems of editing the Diary of Grief aside in order to work on the other two books, but I continued to make occasional diary entries.

Erwin rang from Australia last night. He had just finished reading the Sarah book, which he liked and also found very upsetting. He sobbed over the phone, saying that he felt her death as forcefully as on the first day. 'Those people who say it will get better with time are absolutely wrong. It hasn't faded at all. It's just as terrible now as on that first day.' I had been concentrating on the work of writing, which distanced me from her, but on listening to

Erwin, feeling her close to me through him and through his re-seeing of her through my book, I also felt that nothing can diminish that terrible knowledge. The notion of writing publicly about grief seemed totally absurd. I couldn't convey its intensity, and wouldn't want to.

Conversation with P I told him I had just finished writing a book. What was it about? About myself and my daughter. P asked, 'Is there something special about your daughter?' 'Yes, she's dead.' I replied in a conversational tone. And that's how it has to be. That or nothing. It feels both natural and grotesque, to remain so calm, to demand an equal and unembarrassed response from my listeners. And for once I received it, instead of the familiar rapid changing of the subject, or the comment that it must be good therapy – implying that it can't be much good anything else.

Most of my readers miss the point – that is, my point. Naomi and others: 'I'm much more interested in you than in her.' Janos: 'She was only a child. She wasn't a person.' Margaret: 'What I particularly like is your portrait of family life in Melbourne.' My reaction to these opinions is not 'I've clearly failed,' but 'They are blind'. Julie, alone so far, said, 'I've never read anything which gives such a vivid picture of what a child is like.' She also said that it is worthwhile having taken eighteen years to write it.

I long ago stopped thinking of the book as a 'memorial' to Sarah, after asking what memorials perpetuate. Usually little more than a name. There is a great gulf between the sculpture, the fountain or the garden seat and the person it is said to memorialise. I decided that unless my book could move its readers and change their understanding of children and of life, as she had changed mine, it would be pointless. And I thought I could achieve that by evoking a true sense of Sarah as she had been. Comments by readers have made me see that it doesn't work like that (when it does work.) No-one is going to see Sarah as I do, or respond to her with my exhilaration and love. What has moved readers is some evocation of past happiness with their own children, or sometimes a promise of future happiness with children yet to be born or an insight into parenthood by those who have no children. Not a true apprehension of Sarah, but a few sparks from the radiance of her living self.

Still, after twenty years, I have a feeling of unreality. I can't accept her death as something that has happened, in the nature of things, an experience uniquely mine yet joining me to other survivors. It remains outrageous, it should not have happened, so I can still discover it to be untrue. I seem to be living in some nightmare distorted world behind which the real world still exists, so that some day I might return to it – that is, might find myself back in the world in which she lives. Of course I recognise the absurdity of this delusion. The world is a place where beautiful, lively, deserving and loved five-year-olds can die suddenly, and more brutally than she did. I don't doubt that for a minute. Yet the sense of incongruity persists.

Vanessa Bell, in a letter to her sister Virginia Woolf, describes her efforts to catch and chloroform a huge moth for her son Julian's collection. He was 19 at the time. Then: 'I wish you would write a book about the maternal instinct. In all my wide reading I haven't yet found it properly explored… Of course it is one of the worst of the passions, animal and remorseless.'

I read this with surprised assent, or semi-assent, and the recognition that earlier I would never have countenanced such a sardonic judgment, remembering how affronted I was by Phyllis McGinley. Meditating on Sarah's lifetime made me aware of the irrational excess of my love for her, but I assumed that this maternal passion was beneficent and admirable. Now I'm at least prepared to question it.

'In time, the pain of her death will disappear and only happy memories will remain,' my brother-in-law, André, whose only son was killed in the war, told me. I doubt if I will ever reach that state, but sometimes I catch a glimpse of it. I see us on a spring morning visiting the Sorrento tip, hidden in ti-tree scrub behind the sand dunes, with seagulls wheeling overhead and the surf booming out of sight and Sarah running across the platform of compacted rubbish, intensely and joyfully *there*. A remembered instant which temporarily blots out the anguish of her death.

Sarah's death day, 15th June. I reflected while driving into Soller this morning that I would feel disloyal, if I didn't think about her today.

Later. I replace the paper in the typewriter to add: 'I don't want to let the day pass, my loved daughter, without telling you that I miss you and long for you, that I must speak to you even though I know you cannot hear and are nowhere, and that I still have a faint irrational hope, or perhaps just a pretence of hope, that you do hear.'

Later still. I haven't previously indulged in the fantasy of addressing her directly in this diary. In my first wild private ramblings I often spoke to her, pouring out my love and longing, but I haven't for a long time now. I don't 'really' have the smallest fragment of belief that I could reach her, and the indulgence in make-believe has only rarely seemed permissible. Some elegies for dead children are written entirely in the second person, like a one-sided conversation with the lost child. *The Story of Gabrielle*, which I wrote about in an earlier diary entry, is one that I have admired, reread and studied. But for me to write as if I were speaking to her would seem bitterly ironical.

Typing out the Daniel Diary notes, I feel particularly happy when I come to occasions when he talked confidently about her return. 'When I'm three I'm going to school, and then Sarah will come back from the angels and we'll have lots and lots of bananas and pears and apples to take to school in our paper bags, and we'll go to school together.' Each time, I share his optimism. And last night I dreamed that she was again lying feverish in bed and then, instead of being sent to hospital, recovered.

The Daniel Diary brings back the atmosphere of the days immediately after she died, when she still seemed close, when she was still present in every room of the Power Street house. I have often noticed that a strong sense of happiness, like that of her lifetime, pervades memories of those early days, so that I'm not sure whether the moment I am reliving occurred while she was alive or after her death. I think of a winter outing with Erwin and Daniel to the timbermill at Powelltown, and the memory is imbued with the joy of her presence, like our visit a year earlier to that other timbermill near Marysville, where Sarah and Daniel played together under a flowering wattle tree.

I don't want to get over this obsession with grieving. even now, after twenty years. To have it torn from me would be a repetition of having her torn from me. 'How can you bear to go on writing about that gloomy subject?' Irene asked. But I don't find it gloomy. It is challenging, puzzling and absorbing. And unavoidable.

I have kept the lock of her hair we cut on the morning of her funeral in a beautiful enamelled copper box, which we bought in Florence years ago as a present for my mother. When I opened the box this morning, the gleaming brightness of her hair astonished me. At the time it had seemed a good idea to preserve something that had been physically part of her – a way, I suppose, of keeping her alive. Now it seems worse than useless; I am afraid of it, lurking in the box, ready to spring at me and say, 'She is dead and forgotten. You can't even recall her vividness.' A reminder of how much is lost – the non-anecdotal reality that can't be held in memory.

While writing about her, I have thought of three other girls who died young, but whose lives and personalities have survived: Marjory Fleming, Anne Frank and Marie Bashkirtsev, who died when they were 10, 14, and 25. I want Sarah to join this small band. I want her to be as immortal, as loved and understood, as they are.

But those three survived through their own writing. Scottish Marjorie Fleming left a handful of letters and diaries with an irresistible originality, honesty and charm. Anne Frank's diary has been read by millions. Marie Bashkirtsev, the talented daughter of a well-off Russian family of the *ancien régime,* who died of tuberculosis in 1884, also left diaries, which explore the yearnings and frustrations of a young lady of her time and station, and were a best seller when first published. Three gifted and precocious writers who live on through their own words.

Sarah was not old enough to write, but she was a gifted and precocious talker. I collected up everything I could remember of her talk – not enough to content me, and none of her long, exuberant tellings about what she had just seen, but including some of her vivid personal phrases. Perhaps it will be her own words that most strongly convey a sense of her being to people who never knew her. That she should be known, admired and loved long after she and I are both dead will do no good to either of us. I don't understand why I should want it, but I do, passionately.

I pick up a translation of *The Odyssey* and open it at random – at the arrival of Odysseus in the land of the Cyclops. Immediately I hear Sarah, aged three, demanding 'Read about Polyphemus,' and I see, almost smell, the dining room at Portsea where she was standing, with its fruit-patterned plastic tablecloth, and the vast shining sea beyond the window. I had read her a children's version of the gruesome story of Odysseus and his sailors shut up in a cave by the one-eyed giant Polyphemus, to be eaten two at a time for his dinner, and of their escape by clinging to the bellies of his sheep, after they had blinded him with a blazing stick. She demanded the story again and again. I remember telling John O'Brien, Professor of Ancient History at Melbourne, about this eagerness, and his smile of pleasure at her seeming precocity. But she wasn't revealing an early appreciation of classical myth, only a taste for the macabre.

Another time I made a similar mistake. I had been

reading a life of Ernest Shackleton, and remarked to Erwin on his extraordinary fortitude in the journey across the Antarctic ice-floes 'without losing a single man'. Sarah overheard, and asked about Shackleton with an appearance of lively interest. Always eager to answer her curiosity, I bought a book about him written for children. As soon as I started to read, I could see that I had misinterpreted her interest. She couldn't follow the hazards of Shackleton's expedition, or appreciate the immensity of his achievement. What had caught her interest was simply the reference to death, a focus just then for her terror and fascination.

These diaries record my struggles on the road to finding and resting in the truth. Or so I once hoped. I had a notion of the truth as a resting-place. But it hasn't been so. However often I repeat phrases like 'cosmic indifference', or 'she is dead and I am alive', I continue to appeal against her death, citing notions of justice and her individual gifts. I don't often argue from my own deserts – but sometimes I detect the hint of a plea that there hasn't been all that much happiness in my life and I deserve more than this desolation. Truth hasn't silenced the insistant clamour of longing.

For more than 20 years I have kept a newspaper obituary of Pamela Frankau. I have never read any of her novels, though I did read her autobiography, which tells how she became an author. I kept the cutting for one sentence: 'Her only child died in infancy,' and for the photograph of a writer whose only child died in infancy, and who stares straight ahead through large round spectacles, as if to outface the bitterness of death.

From a piece by Christian McEwen in *Granta*, writing about the deaths of a brother and a sister and his subsequent sense of guilt. 'Everybody had it, fumbling, as if guilt were somehow a relief, easier to admit to than those blazing absences...' – his reaction to lacerating deaths, different to mine. It is his next comment which captured my attention: 'It is difficult to acknowledge that people have their own lives, their own deaths, their own integrity. You cannot save them.

'And that applies even to a five-year-old daughter. From the moment of birth – her own life,' I wrote on first copying this extract. Later, I added: 'The quotation holds a message, but I don't try to define what it is; I simply repeat the words with a sense that they express an important truth.'

I have been reading a new biography, by Stanley Weintraub, of Queen Victoria, who has a place in any catalogue of exemplary grievers, less for the self-pity and self-absorption of which she is often accused, than for the splendid grotesquerie of her efforts to preserve the physical setting of her life with Albert.

For years she would sleep with his nightshirt in her arms. Every night thereafter, she knelt at Albert's side of their bed before she put her head on her own pillow... In each of their homes, his dressing room or study would be kept as it had been, even to the changing of linens, the daily replacement of towels and nightclothes, and – in the dressing rooms – the bringing of hot water for shaving each morning, and a scouring of the unused chamber pot.

It wouldn't get the approval of modern grief therapists, but I admire the flamboyance of a practice that, unless like Brücke we deliberately sweep away all reminders of the dead, most of us follow more modestly.

I enjoy also her brisk dismissal of a clergyman who had written to her, 'Henceforth you must remember that Christ himself will be your husband.' 'That is what I would call twaddle. The man must have known he was talking nonsense. How can people like that comfort others or teach anybody?'

I was interested to learn that she too kept a commonplace book of grief, an 'album consolatium,' into which she entered poems, extracts from prayers and sermons, and observations on widowhood.

Another revelation from a review, this time by Anthony Clare, writing about *The Minimal Self* by Christopher Lasch, who suggests that in the contemporary world, the supreme virtue is survival. 'The survivor seeks to become invulnerable, to protect himself against pain and loss. In this sense, ours is less a narcissistic society than a psychopathic one.' – a condemnation which might well give one a jolt. I have adapted Lasch's words to make a stern motto for myself: 'Acceptance of pain and loss.'

A debate about acceptance has been going on throughout my diaries. The two themes, 'I have at last come to accept' and 'I will never accept' alternate with such monotonous regularity that I call them 'temperature-taking.' With unreliable instruments. I hardly remember what up till now I have meant by acceptance, but certainly it contained the notion that pain would fade, to be replaced by some heroic and morally satisfying renunciation. Suddenly it has become startlingly clear to me that pain and loss must be accepted *as* pain and loss, in all their anguish, and accepted not once but repeatedly. Not any abstract pain and loss, but the pain and loss of *her* death, which will stay with me forever.

I add to my gallery of archetypical grievers Mrs de Valera, encountered in *The Pebbled Shore*, the autobiography of Elizabeth Longford, who writes about the death of her own daughter Catherine:

> I think I have got over it. I am sometimes asked whether faith helped: belief in immortality and a personal resurrection. My answer is that nothing lessens the pain at the time. I remember Frank being sent for by Mrs de Valera, a devout Catholic and wife of the Irish President, soon after Catherine died. 'Tell Elizabeth,' she said to him, 'that I cried

every day for a year when our youngest son was killed in a riding accident. She will do the same. But now I would not have him back.'

'Now I would not have him back.' Another way of resolving grief and perhaps a measure of the power of religious belief. Unavailable to me and unenvied.

In *When the Grass Was Taller,* Richard N. Coe defines what he sees as a separate and increasingly extensive literary genre, the autobiography of childhood, which he calls simply 'the Childhood'. He has read an immense number of such autobiographies, in a wide range of languages, and discusses them with epigrammatic brilliance.

At its ending, the Childhood stretches through adolescence to the threshold of maturity; its beginning reaches back, as a continuous story, to the age of – seven, six, occasionally five. Earlier than that, there is only the isolated vivid memory, without context. The author of a Childhood is writing about himself as a distant and alien persona – it is what distinguishes the genre from the 'standard' autobiography – but he remembers enough of this childish self to compose a narrative. Not enough, though, to include those earliest years. There can be no autobiography of infancy. Only another person can write the story of the first five years, and very few have. Since she died, I have read about early childhood in a variety of genres. There are the classic parental diaries covering a few months of babyhood, and a multitude of professional studies of aspects of infancy, illustrated by narrowly-focussed observations and anecdotes, which don't give, and are not intended to give, the sense of a continuing and growing individual presence. I have read only a tiny handful of accounts covering the first five years of a child's life, or a shorter period, and know of a number of others which I haven't been able to get hold of (e.g. by Elizabeth Gaskell and George Sand). I haven't read any record of those first five years as complete and detailed as mine of Sarah. That won't remain true for long, but it gives me hope that her book might find a publisher.

Alconasser. Sitting at my desk, I looked up and saw an old man outside the door, dressed in shabby brown wool, with a brown wool cap on his head and a bundle of hay on his shoulder. He explained in barely comprehensible *castellano* that he was looking for his sheep. Later I saw him talking to Miguel, and when Miguel came up to the house I asked if they had found the sheep. 'No. There were nine of them and they have been missing for a week. I think they must have been stolen.' I feel the tenderness in that bundle of hay intended to lure back the errant sheep, and the wounding loss if they have really been stolen. Later I learn that the old man is Jeannot, rescuer of lost and crippled and unwanted animals: the sheep, two donkeys, assorted dogs and cats, rabbits and birds. He spends most of his income on food for them.

Writing about Sarah has helped me to see that throughout

her lifetime I floated on an illusion of omnipotence. Although I recognised from her first day that she was a self-contained source of growth and independence and miracle, with her own unique identity unfolding forcefully from within, I also imagined that I possessed absolute power to foster and protect her. She was both separate from me and part of me. For years I could not fully recognise the permanence of her death because I felt her still part of me. ('It is difficult to acknowledge that people have their own lives, their own deaths.') Lately I get nearer to acknowledging separateness. If, as I repeatedly insist, I can't accept her death *for her*, equally I can't refuse to accept it *for her*. It is her fate. Mine too, and Erwin's and Daniel's, but not annihilatingly. Her fate to know, in ideal form, a child's life, with its dependency and limitations, its eager reaching out to the future, and its fullness of love received and given. To love, in Michael Balint's wonderful phrase, 'innocently, unconditionally, as only children can love'. To love with an adult strength of passion and, at the end of five years, to die.

VII

Getting Published
1988 – 1992

I finished a second draft of A Shining Space and a first draft of The Daniel Diary, and at Julie Friedeberger's suggestion sent them both to Anne Charvet at Grafton Books. There followed a very long wait for a decision. Anne thanked me for my patience, but I had no choice. Finally, Grafton offered me a contract to publish The Daniel Diary. I put in a plea that they should first take A Shining Space, about which I felt the more passionate, but to no avail.

After so many years of writing in solitude and secrecy, it was immensely invigorating to work with a skilled professional team. Grafton produced a handsome book that I am proud of, which appeared in May 1988. Because of the unusual subject, I got more coverage on radio and television and in the provincial press than many unknown writers, and thoroughly enjoyed my fifteen minutes of fame. To talk about her and her death publicly and calmly was a relief, and dissipated the air of furtiveness that had hung over the work of writing about her.

A published book exists in a way that no polished and admired and seemingly final typescript does. Publication is a giving-birth. The child must now live its own separate life. To be the parent of this handsome and appealing child gave my confidence an enormous and needed boost – even though at the same time, like every new author, I rapidly lost my optimism about the welcome it would receive from the world. It was never destined to be an instant best-seller, although it might eventually have become a minor classic. But most bookstores appear to have ordered only one or two copies, which soon disappeared. Hatchards in Piccadilly was the only place where I ever saw it in stock, and there, due to the hazards of alphabetical shelving, it was placed high up behind the cash desk, out of reach of casual browsers. And just before a review in the leading bereavement journal appeared, the Grafton accountants removed it from their list.

Meanwhile I revised A Shining Space once again, and the Diary of Grief went on expanding. And I acquired for the first time a friend with whom I could discuss writing, my own and hers, in an informal and colleaguial way. She was Alicja Iwanska, a Polish-American sociologist or, as she would prefer to put it, a Polish sociologist in exile, who was also a novelist, poet and essayist. We had known each other as fellow students of sociology at Columbia University forty years earlier, when we had lived in the same rooming-house. She had recently retired from American academic life and moved to London, where she taught at the Polish University in Exile, and continued to write in various genres. We became each other's confidante, critic and encourager, I only for her sociological work, since her literary writing was in Polish. We differed temperamentally. She wrote rapidly and prolifically, and once a piece was finished became indifferent to criticism, wanting to get it out and be on with the next thing; I tinker endlessly. She had immense self-confidence but appalling English; I had immense self-doubt. We needed and helped each other.

There have been occasions when the illusion that Sarah was still alive somewhere was for a moment so strong that when I look back it seems as if for a short interval she really did live again. As I left the studio of Radio Birmingham after the most intelligent and enjoyable of the interviews that followed publication of *The Daniel Diary,* the interviewer called out in farewell: 'I still think she's up there somewhere.' Briefly, I pictured her 'up there', and felt a rush of joy. And when the moment of conviction passed, there was still pleasure in remembering that I had fleetingly known it.

I showed some of my Diary of Grief pieces to Alicja, the first time anyone has seen any of them. Later she rang to say she wants to encourage me to get on with the book because of its theme, which she defined as how, contrary to accepted notions, atheism can support as well as undermine in grief. But I must think about whether atheism has been a support. Offhand, it seems neither support nor handicap, just there, not chosen but totally accepted, a plain fact of existence.

If the language of earlier bereaved sometime disconcerts,

so does their behaviour. Mary Shelley's bleak journal entry: 'Find my baby dead. Send for Hogg. Talk. A miserable day. In the evening read *Fall of the Jesuits.*'

And the diary of Lady Cynthia Asquith, after hearing that her younger brother had been killed in France:

> Oh how it hurts and how little one ever faced the possibility for an instant! Darling, darling little Yvo – the perfect child and youth. How can one not be going to see him again? None of the others could have quite emptied the future for each of us quite like him... For the first time I felt the full mad horror of war.

But then the very next day:

> I lunched with Guy and Frances. Mamma and Bibs came. Then I went out shopping with Mamma; we bought reach-me-downs at Selfridges...

I sometimes think that I ought to be able to present arguments for non-belief. I don't feel any personal need to, just boredom at the prospect, though it might look more respectable. But I have been reading *The Statue Within*, the autobiography of the French geneticist François Jacob, who, as a child, absorbed various facets of belief from different members of his extended Jewish family, and used to feel particularly proud when he accompanied his strictly observant father to synagogue on the High Holidays. Later he began to turn against extremes of religious fervour. One Yom Kippur he found himself sitting next to a young man 'plunged into a maelstrom of devotion'. Jacob watched his bowings and scrapings and chantings, and his furtive glances to make sure that his piety was being observed.

> Suddenly a question flashed into my mind: 'What if God doesn't exist?' The answer seemed to me plain. Everything – synagogue, rabbis, God, prayer – all this was merely a farce that rolled on from age to age, like an ocean created by the credulity and anguish of men. The heavens were empty. Man was alone. Alone, man did what he could. As best he could.

There is no further mention of religious belief in the autobiography. No arguments, no weighing of evidence, no self-justification. What is good enough for François Jacob is good enough for me!

But it is only while writing this book, facing in imagination the ridicule often poured on non-believers, that I have worried about arguments. I never had much faith to lose, so felt no need to justify its loss. My parents were probably believers in a vague unexamined way, but they were not churchgoers, and I had no religious teaching as a young child. Later I went to a boarding school which was visited on alternate Sundays by the local Church of England vicar and the local Presbyterian minister, two such uncharismatic and unconvincing clerics that my non-belief was not in danger. I was indeed confirmed into the Church of England while at school, and had first to be baptised, but I joined the confirmation class only because I didn't want to be left out. When I learned that the confirmation service was to be in the middle of the half-term holiday and that I would have to go back to school for it, I wanted to drop out, but my mother wouldn't allow it for such a frivolous reason. I have never taken communion since, nor attended a church service except as a curious outsider.

A definition of 'acceptance' by Elisabeth Kübler-Ross: 'A feeling of victory, a feeling of peace, of serenity, of positive submission to things we cannot change.' But I want it to be a memory of burning joy and a state of thankfulness. I want 'How terrible that she died!' to be finally obliterated by 'How wonderful that she was!'

I puzzled for years over the connection between the general law, all men are mortal, and the particular fact that she died so young, the one truth easy to accept, the other immensely difficult and, it seemed to me, totally unconnected to the general law. I argued to myself that 'All men are mortal, but no law says that Sarah Fabian must die at five.' It seemed a valid challenge to the universal law, proof that her death had been a monstrous error, grounds for demanding a retrial. Only recently has a countervailing formula occurred to me: 'No law says that Sarah Fabian is immune from death at five.' An undoubted truth, and one that answers the puzzlement. But not exactly comforting.

Very moved by Allon White's autobiographical fragment

Too Close to the Bone. When White was five, his three-year-old sister Carol drowned in one of the hidden ponds and ancient moats which thread his native village of Cranfield. Many years later, he came to understand that Carol's death had exercised a gloomy unconscious dominance over his imagination as a writer, and over his life.

> Until last year she remained somehow unburied for me. I could not 'put her away', too many unfinished and importuning emotions remained... I set about trying to settle the account with Carol. I needed to rid myself of all that stagnant water and muddy morbidity, shake it off once and for all. I needed to be able to bury her at last, peacefully and permanently. I needed to let go of her...

I copied out this passage because of its many metaphors for the end to mourning, that conclusion which I find questionable, and which Allon White seems to have found difficult to define. His search for a way to exorcise his sister's ghost beckons to me. The farewell had to be symbolic because the real parting had occurred long before. He thought of planting a tree to replace one his father had planted at Carol's birth, which had died.

> It was not enough merely to have this vision. I must actually do it, actually buy a juniper sapling and go back to the old house and plant it as it had been... I dug the hole in the earth, but before I put the tree into it I placed a small wooden box beneath the roots with a rose inside it and a short prayer to Carol asking her to help me. The tree looked beautiful.

A solemn private ritual, a gift, a message, a resurrection – yes, I can see it could be satisfying, but I don't want to emulate him. A final farewell to Sarah is simply impossible, and I don't want it.

Psychoanalysts have recently taken to referring, with irritating knowingness and no explanation, to the 'end of mourning'. For example Winnicott: 'Mourning too tends to finish its job.' I just don't know what he means. The end of mourning is, I suppose, the recognition, so absolute that one no longer fights against it, of utter calamity. Mourning is the struggle *not* to recognise.

But I doubt whether I will ever totally recognise her death. I still have a deep sense that it ought not to be. Like Philip Toynbee, who wrote to Esmond Romilly in 1941 after Romilly had returned from airforce leave to find five of his friends missing:

> I don't think anyone can cope with death – least of all the religious people who think they can. It's monstrous, and impossible to accept or assimilate – or at least I feel that it will always remain so for me. I never feel, well thank God he died as he would have wished. All that matters is that the person no longer exists and that one (and perhaps the world) is worse off without them.

Yes, how I feel. And why do I need someone else's words, instead of speaking in my own voice? It is fellowship and an assurance of rationality to know that my feelings are shared.

That wistful longing for a ritual of remembrance in which I could participate fully occasionally returns. I have glimpsed a model for it in the Japanese festival for the dead, O-Bon, which I read about in two works of fiction. In late summer, the souls of the dead are believed to return to earth. On the last night of their stay, they are lighted back to their spirit-home by little paper lantern-boats, each bearing the name of a dead soul, launched on water and left to drift away into darkness. In Meira Chand's novel *The Bonsai Tree*, Kate and her Japanese husband light a lantern for their still-born son.

> On the far side of the river the great armada of sacred lantern boats were being lit and launched one by one, pushed out into the current. Their flotilla thickened, the lights bobbing and shivering, moving slowly forward, drawn out by the river upon their journey... 'Now,' said Jun, 'Now. Put it into the water.' He bent and lit the small white candle and the lantern came alive. Kate lifted it carefully over the side, and placed it upon the water. Jun leaned out and gave it a push. It floated slowly away into the dark...

And in a short story by Francis King, a Japanese professor whose only son has died describes a village variant of the ceremony.

> They have a cave which they call 'The Cave of the Children's Ghosts' ... The people there – the country people – believe that at this time of the year – during the festival of O-Bon, the Festival of the Dead – all the dead children come back to play in

one of the caves… It's oddly moving, you know. You tell yourself that it's all nonsense, sentimental nonsense. But it – it moves one.

As these descriptions moved me. I took hold of the images, of the children returning to the cave to play with their old toys, of lantern-boats bearing the souls of the loved dead, still near, still close enough to be helped; I envied those for whom such poetic rituals were available. But then I saw that neither writer presents the ceremony as consoling. When it is over, Kate feels a sense of great loneliness, foreseeing the end of her hopeful intimate involvement in Japanese life. Francis King's professor slips away in the darkness while the little lights bob slowly further away, and tries, unsuccessfully, to drown himself.

The *Independent* prints an interview with the survivor of a plane crash in Honduras in which 131 people died, Ron Devereux from Perth, Australia, who, with his wife, Helen, managed to escape from the wreckage alive.

The plane hit something very big and hard. The seats came up out of the floor, luggage fell out of the overhead racks. I knew the next time it hit I was going to die for sure… Little fires were breaking out all over the plane. I could hear people moaning, calling for help. There was a split in the roof just over my head and I reached up and tried to pull it apart, but I couldn't budge it. I saw the fires doubling in size. People were starting to panic.

I had the sudden realisation I was going to be burned alive and I envied the people who were dead. There was a little girl in the aisle seat and the leg of her pants caught fire and she was starting to scream in pain. I rose in my seat and forced the metal aside. I was in such a panic of being burned alive I think I could have run through a brick wall. I broke out onto the roof, [and he succeeded in pulling his wife, who was dazed with shock, out after him.] I could hear the little girl screaming and the fire was further up her clothes. I grabbed her hand and pulled with all my strength but she wouldn't budge... Then the flames started drafting up the hole toward us and I realised there was no possibility of me being able to free her at all and I let her hand go. [Ron and Helen Devereux managed to roll or jump off the roof and haul themselves to a grassy gully before the plane blew up.]

Ron Devereux's words frighteningly depict the last moment in the life of that child, a moment balanced between almost-normality and the nothingness of death, when the outcome might still have been totally different. There are such crises at the end of many lives, at the end of hers, when an emergency tracheotomy was attempted which could have been successful. I cannot think of that moment of balance, for the child in the plane, for her, without feeling a spurt of hope and then, once more, confronting the inexorable void of death.

Another chance-discovered reference to a child's death, this time in a letter from W.E. Henley to Auguste Rodin, written after the death of Henley's five-year-old daughter, Margaret.

> I believe my verses won't all perish. And yet what is the use of speaking about it? I am dead, my wife too is dead. We lost all in losing that marvel of life and wit, our daughter. You would have cared for her too. She had everything, everything.

Is it morbid to seize on such instances of other people's despair almost as avidly as I did at first? I don't think so. They help to confirm the new perspective on the world I have had to discover since she died. As the rituals and texts of established religions demonstrate, beliefs and certainties need to be constantly reaffirmed, and illustrated by new examples.

Forthright recommendations of non-belief are rare. Until now, the only one in my repertoire of maxims has been Brecht's 'Grosser Dankchoral'. So I welcome Salman Rushdie in the *Independent* a few days ago.

> I would like to say this: life without God seems to believers to be an idiocy, pointless, beneath contempt. It does not seem so to non-believers. To accept that the world, here, is all there is, to go through it, towards and into death, without the consolations of religion seems, well, at least as courageous and rigorous to us as the espousal of faith seems to you.

GETTING PUBLISHED

I am heartened by Rushdie's affirmation, and repeat it to myself, though I keep forgetting his choice of adjectives and have to look them up: 'courageous and rigorous'. I would have liked him to add 'exhilarating and strengthening'.

Last Sunday, with Alicja to give me moral support, I took *The Daniel Diary* to a Book Fair. We authors were each given a table in an open-fronted marquee, where I set up my piles of copies and a poster Erwin had designed, while Alicja surveyed the offerings of other exhibitors and reported that there was scarcely a single work of literature among them, only how-to books and stories for children.

After a poor and expensive lunch, I stood for two hours in the icy draught that blew under the canvas, while people filed past, glanced at the poster with its reproduction of the book jacket – 'A unique insight into the mind of a very young child as he confronts tragedy', and moved on, unstirred by any desire to share that confrontation. '*I* couldn't cope with the death of a child,' the woman at the next table, who was doing a brisk trade in children's books, said sanctimoniously, as if someone as sensitive could never be in the position of bloody well having to.

I sold just one copy, to a young woman in a hat who had looked round the entire fair before deciding what to buy, and who carried off her purchase with a pleased smile. We left early, but I felt that the foray had been doubly worthwhile. I want *The Daniel Diary* to be received as a book for everyone, not just for the bereaved, but I was given the salutary lesson that only a tiny proportion of 'everyone' will have the slightest desire to read it. And I brought away a vivid image of one person who looked forward excitedly to that reading.

My habit, since Sarah died, of collecting and repeating verbal formulae (maxims, texts, precepts, sayings) has lead me to an interest in theories about the role of formulae in pre-literate societies, their transformation with the invention of writing and then of print, and their survival today. Walter Ong in *Orality and Literacy*:

> An oral culture has no texts. How does it get together organized material for recall? ... The only answer is: Think memorable thoughts ... You have to do your thinking in mnemonic patterns, shaped for ready oral recurrence. Your thought must come into being in heavily rhythmic, balanced patterns, in repetitions or antitheses, in alliterations and assonances, in epithetic and other formulary expressions ... in proverbs which are constantly heard by everyone so that they come to mind readily and which themselves are patterned for retention and ready recall, or in other mnemonic form.

My mottoes have some of these characteristics, and for the same reason – they can be easily retained and instantly recalled, without the delay of looking them up in books. Often I didn't note them down when I first came upon them – there was no need. Some are memorable formulations of what I had already thought, or half thought. A few, like 'acceptance of pain and loss', jolted me suddenly into new awareness.

Formulae like those of oral cultures haven't totally disappeared from our highly literate societies. They survive in the form of proverbs, famous sayings, well-known quotations, slogans, catch-phrases, advertising jingles. But I have never seen any study of what they do for us in our personal lives today, or how we use them, nor found any personal report, other than an occasional passing reference – Tony Benn in a radio programme saying that he had always tried to abide by the adage 'Never let the sun go down on your wrath.' My impression is that although people still repeat proverbs and standard sayings (though not nearly as often as their grandparents did), they don't shape lives, but are part of what Roland Barthes scathingly calls the doxa, received wisdom, unexamined and profoundly boring, a sort of social insulation. As they already were for Shakespeare, with his Polonius-figures 'full of wise saws and modern instances'. No-one's day is deeply influenced by the quotation on his desk calendar. I don't trot out my formulae in conversation; they are private mnemonics. How many other secret formula-addicts are out there, I don't know.

Counting my blessings – Sarah's life and the years of mourning for her. Gratitude for both. If I can't have her continuing life, I am glad to have the wrestle with her death.

What we lost, Erwin and Daniel and I, is immeasurable; our lives are irreparably diminished. But I, at least, have also gained – a purpose in life, an avocation, an occupation, an achievement. I have written two books, the best I could do, and far better than anything I could have produced at the time she died. Her death saved me from failure. Already before she was born I had dropped out of academic life, though I hadn't recognised the fact. I still aspired to write a sociological masterpiece, and had ideas on which I worked enthusiastically, but without enough loyalty to counter the facts that my livelihood didn't depend on making something of them, and that no-one was encouraging me, or pressing for results. Living in a fantasy-world, a withdrawal that would have been hard, i.e. impossible, to reverse. What I pride myself now on having achieved, I owe to her. To her life and her death.

An ache of sorrow for three children drowned in a canal, and especially for the youngest, 8 months, who fell in while his mother was trying to save his older sisters. So many lives abruptly ended; immensities of future experience suddenly obliterated. I remember objecting fiercely when Hugo said, soon after Sarah died, that mourning was regret for what *might have been*. I mourned what *was*, a life reaching back into the past and forward into the future, something totally different from free-floating dreams of might-have-been. I have been haunted all day by the thought of that mother's relentless knowledge that if she had spent a few seconds making sure the baby was safe, then he at least would still be alive.

Approaching the end of re-writing A Shining Space and typing it onto my new computer leaves me feeling abandoned and desolate. I have 'finished' it three times now, and every ending has been a new bereavement. Once more she is engulfed by the void. I lose the companionship with her that I had during the years of writing, and the sense of still being able to do something for her.

Although I worked on the book, intermittently, for almost thirty years, it is written by the person I was when she died, out of the unquestioned sense of wonder and miracle that I had during her lifetime. I was not much interested in other children while she lived, or in theories about parenthood or child development. We felt, we lived, as if we were the only ones, never such blessedness, and that is how I have written. A few reflections that did not occur to me while she was alive have crept in, but very few. Her portrait has the naivety of recent experience, not the detachment of later reflection, and that is how I want it to be.

I reread a newspaper cutting of an interview with Rabbi Lionel Blue, which I have kept because it is full of commonsensical remarks; clichés perhaps, but they can be welcome too. Apropos his homosexuality, 'If I could have changed it, I think I would. But it's like being Jewish. You're landed with it, and there's not much you can do. And then you make the best of it. And then you find that with the hand that's dealt you, you can use that also to grow in love and compassion and generosity, and all those sorts of things…'

Yes, make the best of the hand that has been dealt me. Dealt her too, though she can't make anything of it, good or bad, nor I for her. No use saying to the Great Croupier, 'I won't have that card, deal me another.' The hand has been dealt and there is nothing to do but make the best of it. All this is obvious, but I need to hear it repeated again and again, in different words, by different people, in different tones of voice. Today, as on the day I cut out the interview, I read Lionel Blue's words with gratitude.

I dreamed last night that I held Sarah as a baby in my arms, although the surroundings were strange and Daniel was already there. I have lately had several dreams of her. They don't have much story; she is just there, sometimes as a baby, sometimes as the five-year-old she became. Each time I wake up pervaded by a lost emotion, the radiant, privileged, joyful, and blindly accepted mutual love I knew when she was alive. I re-experience the plenitude of living in the small world of my two beautiful lively children and their loving father. In waking life I have become used to a diminished existence and seldom recall the moods of that time, or the full presence of her living self. Never glad confident morning again. The resurrection of past happiness is an enormous and seldom-recognised gift of dreaming.

An unimpugnable orthodoxy – that mourning is shaped by the experiences of early childhood. OK, but I've never wanted to follow up that line. Her death was an immense cataclysm that came from outside and remained external and obdurate. It changed me and the world in which I lived. I remember my chagrin at discovering, several years after she died, that ancient habits of self-doubt still hampered me in writing, even about her. Nothing should have remained the same, and indeed at first the task of homage seemed totally unlike any other work I had ever undertaken. Fate had imposed on me an absolute duty, which I accepted unquestioningly, and both welcomed and feared. I felt strengthened to deal with it, and so I was. Despite the intrusion of doubts about my ability to write a tribute worthy of her, I worked on doggedly for years, with a persistence I had never known before. The encounter with a terrible and implacable reality was vastly more powerful than any echo of childhood emotion.

Reading another Holocaust story, that of Henry Orenstein, I feel a surge of revulsion against living in a world where men and women can behave with such terrible savagery towards their fellow humans. Orenstein was saved through intelligence and determination as well as luck, but there were times when he too lost the desire to live. Many events in the modern world prompt such a reaction. But to insist that 'I don't want to live in a world in which a child of five can die of a fever' would be absurd. No-one has ever known any other world.

In the early years after she died I used to read books about the Holocaust and about Hiroshima, with the vague urgent hope of finding a truth to illuminate her death. I studied stories by survivors, asking how they managed to live with their searing knowledge, and whether they had 'recovered'. But survivors are reticent about the deepest problems of their afterlives, and only an occasional passing remark linked my story to theirs.

Yet their experience of unthinkable extremes of suffering, terror, grief and endurance helped me to place her death in the brutal real world, instead of seeing it as a grotesque nightmare. However sacrilegious, however lacking in a sense of proportion, we make free use of others' sufferings to understand our own lives. By now the comparison works the other way – awareness of the persistent desolate nothingness of her death helps me to understand the enormity of other people's tragedies and the depth of their suffering.

Struggling with the problems of making a book out of my Diary of Grief notes, I repeat two sayings of Goethe. 'How can a man come to know himself? Never through contemplation, but through action. Try to do your duty, and you will know at once what you amount to.' And what does he mean by duty? Not a conventional task imposed from outside. 'Duty means loving that which one makes imperative upon oneself.' The translations (not mine) sound clumsy, but I can't try to improve them because the London Library copy of *The Permanent Goethe*, edited by Thomas Mann, where I discovered them, has since been lost, and I don't know where to find the originals. Goethe, of all my adopted mentors, is the most severe. Turning my diaries of grief into A Diary of Grief is a duty I have imposed upon myself and, if I fail, then the ineluctable verdict will be that I am the person who cannot write that book.

I meditated on Goethe's precepts while working on the Sarah book too. Eventually I finished it to the best of my abilities, and with satisfaction at having done that much. So I am not, as at times I feared, the person who could not write a book about her. But I *am* the person who could write a book only as good as it turned out to be. It is not the compelling incandescent revelation of her essential self and its miraculous unfolding which I aspired to write. I came to refer to that ideal as 'The Shining Testament', and its unattainable perfection inhibited me on many days from writing anything at all. And it is not even the insightful account that someone more perceptive and with a better memory might have written. But it is the best of which I am capable.

From a book review: 'Since the pioneer work of Philippe Ariès, historians have written hundreds of books and articles about death, covering evidence of every kind, demographical, medical, iconographical, literary, folkloric, and including the analysis of the innumerable Christian works of spirituality on preparation for dying.' Some of these hundreds I have read. I tell myself that if I am going to write about grief I should read more. But almost none of those scholarly works (including Ariès) has done anything for me. No point in reading more. The words which took hold of me, which startled, enlightened and sustained, were mostly found by chance, in unexpected places. I'm not trying to write a treatise on grief, only to describe my own experience; not to produce a balanced anthology, but to share words and examples that have a personal meaning for me.

Peter Noll, in the diary *In the Face of Death*, which he kept while he was dying of cancer, says that only the exemplary person should write about dying. Or, no doubt, about grief. 'His experiences, his way of describing them, his view of contemporary events, and his evaluation of what he is reading must make visible the general through the medium of the individual.' But how can you know that? You can't. It will be for readers to decide – if ever I get published. Besides, simple exemplariness is boring. There has to be something quirky and individual before we notice and remember. As in Philip Toynbee's journals about his search for God, which are lightened by his self-aware buffooneries, or in Peter Noll's accounts of conversations with eminent friends, and his elegaic last visits to the Swiss mountains.

There is one limitation to the exemplariness of all published personal stories about confronting life's worst ordeals. Their authors, including Peter Noll and me, are privileged. We have faithful friends, intellectual resources, time, money, access to the best medical advice, beautiful surroundings, a loving and supportive marriage, a happy family, surviving children – not all of these privileges for any one author, but some combination of them which invites the response, 'It's all very well for her…'

I began the morning with a feeling of revulsion at the prospect of spending the coming months working on a book about my ill-read, self-centred, indolent self. Now, several working hours later, I am again exhilarated by my immense good fortune at being able to sit here at my desk, undisturbed, free to explore themes, ideas, memories – and myself.

My other two books were tributes to them, to Sarah and Daniel. They are also about me, but I don't mind that because the behaviour I describe seemed inevitable and basically right. I could and should have done no other. And I remain convinced of that despite knowing that everyone's behaviour is at times distorted and rendered destructive or futile by their own past history and blind desires. In other contexts I see that I am no exception. But they showed me how to behave by their love and energy, and I listened through love of them. When they were small, and their world relatively uncomplicated. But I don't know whether this long-drawn-out obsession with her death is right or not. I only occasionally ask, and then don't know how to answer. It feels unavoidable.

From a a load of books which Naomi Lewis asked me to store while her flat was being renovated, I picked out a tattered paperback collection of essays by Kierkegaard. It includes a meditation on one of 'the great necessary sayings... one whose beauty and brevity has made it into a proverb', that of Job: 'The Lord gave and the Lord hath taken away. Blessed be the name of the Lord.'

Kierkegaard, in his wordy way, points out that before the Lord took, he first gave, and that Job acknowledges this priority. And I discovered that this famous verse is often misquoted, even by the clergy (and by me, earlier). Job did not say, 'The Lord giveth and the Lord taketh away,' blunting the sharpness of reality by turning it into a generalisation. He said, 'The Lord *gave*... ' It is the truth of a particular loss, our own, my own, which is so hard to acknowledge. And which carries the consolation that before fate capriciously took away, fate capriciously bestowed, on me and on her, a time of miraculous joy and revelation. Her life was neither my desert nor my creation. And if I manage sometimes to add, 'Blessed be the name of the Lord,' it is because I also succeed in acknowledging this unmerited priority. As Cecily did when she exclaimed 'How wonderful that she was!'

I don't reject the deist language. It doesn't lead me to imagine some personal god-figure who orders this giving and this taking away. The time-hallowed metaphor links me with sorrowing multitudes over the centuries, in words whose majestic sonority no rationalist formulation could rival.

Soon after rediscovering Job's testimony, I came across another statement of the same truth, by Schopenhauer, translated in *A Book of Consolations*, edited by P.J. Kavanagh.

> Remember that chance, which (together with error its brother, folly its aunt, and wickedness its grandmother) is the ruling power on this earth and embitters the life of every son of earth, remember, I say, that it is this mischievous power to which you owe your well-being and independence, for it gave to you what it denied to many thousands, just to be able to give it to individuals like you. If you remember this, you will not act as though you had a right to the possession of that for which you are thanking it. On the contrary, you will know that you have all this through the favour of a fickle mistress. Therefore, when she is in the mood to take back from you some or all of these things, you will not raise a hue and cry about her injustice, but you will realise that chance took what chance had given. If needs be, you will observe that it is not quite so favourable to you as it hitherto seemed to be.

I want both these versions. Schopenhauer's idiom is more

modern but less memorable. I look up his piece from time to time, but I don't need to consult a text before repeating 'The Lord gave and the Lord hath taken away.'

Four years later I add an elliptical third version, from André Comte-Sponville:

> 'C'est pas juste,' dit le petit enfant – et de fait cela ne l'est pas. Simplement le bonheur ne l'est pas d'avantage, et ne s'en soucie point.
> 'It's not fair,' says the child – and it certainly isn't. But happiness isn't fair either, and no-one complains about that.

Alicja was here to lunch. We talked about our good fortune in having work to do in our seventies, and about the necessary solitude of writing, and I shared some of my maxims with her. Including, from Rousseau, 'Je sais bien que le lecteur n'a pas grand besoin de savoir tout ceci, mais j'ai besoin, moi, de le lui dire.' [I know perfectly well that the reader has no great need to know all this, but I have a need to tell him.] Erwin, when I shared it with him, applauded this pronouncement, which he sees as an essential attitude for anyone to succeed as a creative artist. You need an egotistical toughness.

And Primo Levi's engineering metaphor in *The Monkey's Wrench*: '... the pleasure of seeing your creature grow, beam after beam, bolt after bolt, solid, necessary, symmetrical, suited to its purpose.' Can I say that about *A Shining Space*? Yes, beam after beam and bolt after bolt, solid and self-supporting, (more or less!). But beyond that, not more than – economical, workmanlike and in scale with my talents, the best I can do. Yet I can imagine with Primo Levi, whose modesty is more appropriate to me than to him, that 'perhaps it will live longer than I do, and perhaps it will be of use to someone I don't know, who doesn't know me. And perhaps in old age I will look back and it will seem beautiful, and then it won't really matter so much that it seems beautiful only to me.'

From Kavanagh's introduction to *A Book of Consolations*: 'In ultimate situations – "At last, the distinguished thing," said the dying Henry James – it is grandeur we need to be assured of; we know the pettiness.' For the dying or for the survivors? The survivors not only need, but get, a sense of grandeur. Death imposes an atmosphere of awe and significance. One walks around feeling above and beyond all the petty concerns of existence. Only the immense juxtaposition of living and dying seems to matter. There were brief moments, in the days immediately after she died, when her death appeared majestically inevitable and my only possible response a proud stoicism.

'We have art that we may not perish of the truth', an

aphorism of Nietzsche's which I have only recently discovered. I look at my collection of sayings in its light. I didn't adopt every relevant or true statement that I encountered or invented, only those which gave me a shock of surprise, often because of their elegance or economy or originality of expression. Miniature works of art. I don't think these qualities prettify or negate truth. Style concentrates their meaning, and makes them easier to remember and to contemplate. Yes, but these epigrammatic sayings also divert attention from painful reality to themselves. All this prolonged effort of reading and searching and meditating on examples and trying to write as well as I can about her and Daniel and myself has been a domestication of truth. But what else? Should I stare forever, in paralysed horror, at the void? Should I try not to think at all about her death, and consequently not about her? Neither of those alternatives!

'How futile it is to try to discover an appropriate response to either a single death or a hundred and thirty-five thousand.' This sentence leaped out at me from a book review by Susan Lardner in *The New Yorker*. It seemed to announce a profound truth, though I copied it without comment. I must have seen an acknowledgment of the complex immensity of response to a deeply-felt encounter with death. So many thoughts and emotions, often contradictory, and all inadequate, either singly or together.

In the end, what changes my view of the world and her place in it is simply the fact. Today, the anniversary of her death, I no longer want to think about what she might have become. I can't even imagine her alive beyond that date. She is that far-off child who lived for only five years. Her mystery dries up.

Two rhymes have haunted me recently:
>And have not little children gone,
>And Lesbia's sparrow, all alone?
>(Oliver St John Gogarty)

And:
>The twelvemonth and a day being up,
>The dead began to speak.
>'Oh who is this sits on my grave,
>And will not let me sleep?'
>(Anon)

Some time ago I clipped a newspaper item about a Dutch therapist who claimed to 'cure' grief in a single day by relentlessly confronting his patients with the facts of their bereavement. I can't find the cutting, but I have been reading *Healing Pain*, by two Danish psychotherapists, Nini Leick and Marianne Davidsen-Nielsen, who practise, with groups and, more gently, a similar method. They present the chronic mourner with plain truths stated in plain language, and ask her to rephrase them and say them back to the group. 'John is dead. You will never see him again. You will never lie beside him in bed again.'

They also employ one of the few modern rituals of grief that can be considered with any respect – the letter of farewell to the dead, which each member, before leaving the group, must write and read aloud. The examples they present are varied and moving, but there is something not quite acceptable about the concept. It is based on the idea of closure, dear both to therapists and members of lay support groups, which I have begun to reject. And it embodies a contradiction – a final acknowledgment of the fact of death addressed to the dead person as if she could read and understand.

The authors praise the healing power of tempestuous weeping.

> The deeper his weeping becomes, the more releasing it is… In deep sobbing there is an acceptance that all hope of seeing the dead one again is over… It may be said that profound weeping contains a letting-go of the dead person.

The group sessions included a good deal of weeping, which spread contagiously. It is an aspect of their treatment which has some appeal for me. Perhaps in such a group I too would have wept profoundly, as I have never done, and felt liberated and grateful. I have been occasionally tempted by accounts of 'grief workshops' – but never with enough conviction to sign up for one.

Healing Pain stirred up a recurrent fear that my journals will be seen as evidence of pathological mourning, a morbid refusal to let go. A craven fear, since from very early on I rejected the division of grief into the normal and the pathological. Professionals may need that distinction, but I don't. My broodings may be unusually long-drawn-out, but they are genuine and mine, one human way of responding to an immense and complex loss. And I am a fervent go-it-aloner, and see in the ubiquitous and eager advocacy of counselling a contempt for the resilience of the independent human spirit.

An interview in *El País* with Leonardo Sciascia, in which he named Pirandello, Kafka and Borges as the three most influential writers of our century, because of their vision of the world. When the interviewer objected that all three were sceptical and negative – not one was a writer with hope, Sciascia replied :

> Su esperanza reside en el hecho de escribir. Porque no hay pesimismo que sea definitivo cuando se escribe. El escribe es siempre un acto de esperanza. Their hope lies in the act of writing. No pessimism is final for the writer. Writing is always an act of hope.

I wrote the Sarah book with a tangle of hopes: to preserve the miracle of her existence by sharing it with other people; to give birth to her again; to continue my companionship with her; to find a use for the restless energy of grief; to create a structure complete in itself; to redeem my own life from past futility; to gain recognition for my talents; to break out of isolation. And, in Stuart

Hampshire's words, out of 'the overwhelming need to communicate one's own individual experience, to add something distinctive to the always growing sum of the evidences of life.' Some of these hopes have been fulfilled, but unfulfilled hopes also have a positive role in life.

I fasten on a short poem in the *Oxford Book of German Verse* by Uhland, the German romantic poet admired by Wittgenstein for his simplicity and reticence.
Du kamst, du gingst mit leiser Spur,
Ein flücht'ger Gast im Erdenland;
Woher? wohin? Wir wissen nur:
Aus Gottes Hand in Gottes Hand.
You came, you went, with a light step, A fleeting guest upon the Earth; Whence? And where to? We only know: From out God's hand, into God's hand.
Another version of the Job consolation. One cannot have too many. And I keep it, as I do that of Job, for its economy and deftness.

She dead and I alive. A grossly unequal relationship, hardly a relationship at all, and yet mysterious. I brood on it often. And today I happened to see two pictures in which the living and the dead are juxtaposed for contemplation. One was a painting by Rembrandt of a young girl, certainly alive although her expression was impassive, and two handsome glittering peacocks, dead, although their plumage gleams. The second, perhaps influenced by that particular Rembrandt, was a drawing by Edward Ardizzone, *Brew-up in North Africa 1942,* depicting a burial party during an unofficial truce. Three young soldiers, one with a chubby face like the girl in the Rembrandt, gaze over their mugs of tea at two dead soldiers laid in a grave but not yet covered over.

The two pictures seem to comment on my preoccupation. But is there anything to be said about what divides the living from the dead, except banalities? I don't think so. The meaning I find in contemplating those images is a case of what can't be said. But both artists chose the subject deliberately.

Just back from a group walking holiday in Sicily followed by four solitary days of entranced enjoyment in Rome, during all of which time I scarcely thought of her, and never with acute grief. I was continually occupied, and usually in pleasant company. Happy, I would judge. But I am left with a feeling of shallowness. I don't want to live like that all the time. Getting back to the work of making a book out of my journals means a return to grieving and longing and the confusions of mourning. But it is also a return to awareness of her continuing existence in my life, she who loved me without reservation, and whom I love equally in return.

Images of Rome still glow. The Via Giulia, laid out in

1508 as the chief thoroughfare from the city to the Vatican, but now a deserted alley between high walls of darkened brick overhung by trees – still the Rome of a time when great cities were more intimate and not yet severed from the countryside. And the mosaic in Santa Maria in Trastevere, where, on either side of Christ in Majesty, the sheep line up 'one behind the other' (a favourite phrase of Sarah's) to enter the Holy City. The metaphor is appealing, as it often is ('All we like sheep...' 'The hungry sheep look up...'). I have a tempting vision of abandoning personal responsibility, and going up into the City of the Father, meekly following the person in front, bearing nothing but my own woolly coat.

I realise some time later that I conflated two memories. That particular mosaic is in Ravenna, not in Trastevere!

I continue to collect grotesque deaths. In the last few weeks: two teenagers asphyxiated in their cabin on an overnight ferry by gases from the ship's malfunctioning sewage system; a sixteen-year-old thrown off a swing when the rope broke; a university student asphyxiated by a faulty gas fire in her college room; a man trimming a hedge who slipped on wet grass and cut his throat with his shears; an Indian child snatched out of a National Park tourist bus by a tiger. And if the last two get close to the farce of Man Killed by Dog, the laughter dries up with my final case: three children in besieged Sarajevo who had been kept in a cellar all day, and then were killed by a mortar shell when they were allowed out to play during the evening lull. All, like her, suddenly swept from life by unpredictable and undeserved chance.

I discovered recently that I am not alone in this obsession; lists of extraordinary and unpredictable deaths were common in Renaissance compilations and handbooks, including one by Montaigne:

> Leaving aside fevers and pleurisies, who would ever have thought that a Duke of Brittany was to be crushed to death in a crowd, as one was during the state entry into Lyons of Pope Clement, who came from my part of the world. Have you not seen one of our kings killed in sport? And was not one of his ancestors killed by a bump from a pig? Aeschylus was warned against a falling house; he was always on the alert but in vain: he was killed by the shell of a tortoise which slipped from the talons of an eagle in flight… And if I may include a personal example, Captain Saint-Martin, my brother, died at the age of twenty-three while playing tennis; he was felled by a blow from a tennis-ball just above the right ear. There was no sign of bruising or of a wound. He did not even sit down or take a rest, yet five or six hours later he was dead from an apoplexy caused by that blow.

Kings and great men provide Montaigne's examples. In the absence of newspapers with their *faits divers*, they were doubtless the ones he knew about, but there is an undertone of surprise and perhaps assuagement in observing that absurd fates await even kings. I have sometimes taken note of the deaths of children of the eminent, out of some need for reassurance that no privileged group is immune from a fate like hers, but I haven't listed them, here or privately, from shame at finding solace in the grief of identified others. My grotesque deaths are anonymous and I hope no survivor will learn how I have used their personal tragedy.

Words that might seem basic to any talk about sudden death, sometimes, even now, surprise me. Lately the word 'random' has cropped up repeatedly. David Cannadine, for instance, speaking in an interview about the cot-death of his baby daughter Harriet, said, 'It has left me with a permanent sense of the random risk of catastrophe in life.' I don't think I have ever used that word; instead I have talked of 'chance' or 'fate', and of 'grotesque' deaths. Now I worry at 'random' like a dog at a bone. Yes, plainly, disaster is in some sense random; catastrophe falls unpredictably, without rhyme or reason, anywhere, on anyone. And yet the concept 'random' is slippery. It seems to mean something different depending on whether it refers to an event that has happened or one that might happen. The random catastrophe that could befall us, although so far it hasn't, could be anything at all, and might happen at any time or might not. But a random death that has occurred is certain, and can be more or less fully understood, its causes explained. There remains only a small gap which leads us to ask 'Why me?', often a detail in the link of causation which, it seems, might have been different. If only he had stepped off the pavement two seconds later! 'Random catastrophe' may help us feel we understand what has happened, but it doesn't help us to face the future. 'Expect the unexpected', or 'Don't take your good fortune for granted', can at most foster a vague sense of lurking insecurity.

I've often joined in the debate about whether grief is for one's own losses or for those of the dead, though plainly it is both. And I am touched to see a reference to a third possibility, in an article on humanist attitudes to death: 'If a young, fit person dies, then ... to realise that we must all manage without the unique contribution that person could have made to society ... may border on the unbearable.' It seems like the particular expression of sorrow for *her* death which I so rarely hear. I think of the many people who in the course of a long life would have been blessed by her radiance. It was for them that I undertook to write her life. My initial resolution was altruistic, though not purely so. I needed an aim large enough to match the significance of her death. Cecily said, 'It will fill us in on the part of her life we missed because you went to Australia.' 'Us' – the few who had known her. It wasn't a grand enough aim. I wanted to reach a much larger audience with a vision of her human stature, and of the stupendous and often unrecognised achievements of early childhood.

In my long-drawn-out wrestlings to believe the plain fact of her death, I come at last to see the imbecile and stubborn optimism of the comfortably insulated *bourgeoise*. I lived the first half of my life protected from direct personal experience of suffering and injustice, and any awareness that such are the common human lot was acquired second-hand. Yes, I had love-affairs that ended badly and left me feeling miserable but, as Colette says somewhere, such betrayals should not be regarded as tragic. But instead of acknowledging that her premature death is one among millions, I persist in seeing it as an unprecedented outrage. It SHOULD not have happened. No-one ever warned me that utter disaster could descend on ME. So I remain astonished and disbelieving.

'The energy released by a death' – another addition to my repertoire of phrases. 'Grief is the energy released by a death' – Adam Mars-Jones in a review. Enormous energy – the energy of panic searching, I suppose, as if the adrenalin of crisis keeps flowing for years. I have stuck at writing and thinking about her until I have almost completed three books. Before her death, I took up, one after another, various promising topics about which I read widely and wrote copious notes – and which I then abandoned before I had produced anything organised and shareable. Grief gave me the energy of doggedness.

I have come across many examples of the energy of the bereaved. I remember especially a TV programme about an American couple whose teenage son disappeared while on a trip to Canada with a friend. To the police he was just another missing kid who might never be traced. The parents mustered enormous resources of persistence, intelligence, time and cash, starting from the single clue of a credit-card purchase of gas, to find his murdered body in a roadside grave, and then to identify his killers and bring them to justice, in the face of official and unofficial indifference and obstruction.

The energy of panic searching! But the bereaved have also had the energy to rebuild, restore, redeem, to change the world in a way symbolically related to the death they mourn – to buy hospital equipment, set up a skin bank, establish a fund for grants to nurses, campaign to change traffic laws and attitudes to reckless driving, to work tirelessly in a thousand different causes.

I am reading a favourite book, *Images and Shadows*, the autobiography of Iris Origo, and vicariously enjoying her privileged life, spent in the ravishingly beautiful Tuscan countryside, and encompassing an enduring marriage, enviable friendships and much generous hard work. Iris Origo, too, lost a beloved child, and in her sorrow turned to writing. But she wrote little about grief, or about her son, Gianni, who died at the age of seven. The idea of devoting the rest of her life to such subjects would have appalled her, though she did write about another doomed child, Byron's ill-used daughter Allegra. And there is a short piece at the end of the autobiography about remembering her beloved dead – her father who died when she was seven, Gianni, and her friend Elsa Dallolio.

> ... though I have never ceased to miss my father, child, and friend, I have also never lost them. They

have been to me, at all times, as real as the people I see every day, and it is this, I think, that has conditioned my whole attitude both to death and to human affection ... My own personal experience has given me a very vivid sense of the continuity of love, even after death ... It is this feeling that has made death seem to me not less painful, never that – for there is no greater grief than that of parting – but not, perhaps, so very important...

She doesn't dwell on anguish or protest. Her summing-up impresses me as noble, exemplary, and moving, as does her record of service to others carried on despite personal tragedy. But Iris Origo belongs to another society and another time. Her attitude is no more possible for me than mine for her. And almost at once I start worrying at her words. 'The continuity of love, even after death' is something I also feel, but not always. 'How wonderful that she was' gets swamped by 'How terrible that she died'. And though Sarah continues to glow in my mind, I could not say truthfully that she is as real as the people I see every day. But then it must be an exaggeration for Origo too, a hyperbolic turn of speech. The living constantly renew themselves by unanticipated doings and sayings, by being there afresh. Immensely different from a beloved inner image. And children are constantly changing, but the dead child is stilled at the moment of death. My occasional fancies of what Sarah would be like as a lover or a mother are vague and thin. I do have a sense of the warmth of love and companionship that she would still offer me, but it doesn't provide the unquestionable thereness of reality, only the fleeting solace of imagining what might have been.

Sometimes, still, a phrase leaps out like a revelation, and I repeat it to myself for days. This time from Peter Noll: 'the cruelty of death, its dark incomprehensibility'. Both he and I are opposed to anyone who wants to smooth away the pain of grief with consoling falsities. Dark incomprehensibility and cruel unfairness belong to death and cannot be exorcised.

Rosemary Dinnage, looking over her collection of interviews about death in *The Ruffian on the Stair*, concluded that in these days of retreat from organised religion, people make up 'their own vague but indispensable structures of belief and ritual.' A neat summary which I have adopted and adapted: 'I have made up my own ramshackle structure of belief and ritual.' And I add a third element, scripture, a concept I take from Rabbi Lionel Blue: 'Most of the people you talk to have no scriptures at all.' That was me when she died. Since then I have been putting together my own 'ramshackle structure of belief, ritual and scripture'. Like all scriptures, mine is a motley accumulation of statements of belief, texts for meditation, stories of heroes, villains and exemplars, phrases that console or reprove, affirmations of the nature of reality, etc. Texts to companion, illuminate and strengthen, to reread, and (some of them), to repeat, as believers ritually repeat their creeds.

By now, 25 December 1992, I have paid my debt to her insofar as I can. It has taken a very long time. I keep a corner of love, longing and protest, but I should be able to allow myself to get on with life, with doing and enjoying, without thinking that I owe it to her to remain reluctant and backward-looking.

VIII

New Texts
1993-1994

Towards the end of 1992 I sent the latest draft of A Shining Space to a new string of agents and publishers. Still no-one wanted to take it on, but again I received a number of sympathetic and thoughtful letters, showing that some publishers do have a heart. Several gave detailed reasons for their rejection, usually to do with sadness. Julia MacRae added:

> There is also the inescapable fact that this lovely child, so vital in all her responses, is known in advance by the reader to be doomed to a cruelly short life, so that all the interesting developments with reading and speech and emotional growth are not, ultimately, going to reach any conclusion – the usual 'point' of books about childhood.

She is right, it is a downer, but the usual point doesn't have to be my point. No life is justified simply by 'reaching a conclusion'. Its value is in the living. That is as true for a child as for an octogenarian. Sarah's achievements of speech and emotional discovery and reading remain triumphs of the human spirit, even though they were not to be built on and transformed over the years. I want others to share that sense of triumph, and see it as something whose worth endures, despite the brevity of her life. The life of a child who dies at five, Sarah's life, is not made up of the experiences she will never know, but of those she knew. There is inevitable sadness in recounting her life, but there is also a great deal of joy.

Literary agents gave different reasons for questioning the book's prospects. Its author is unknown, the story lacks drama, and there is nothing extreme or exotic about the setting. It has no publicity value. I understand these handicaps, but I'm not giving up the attempt to find a publisher. Temporarily, though, I did give up, deciding to put the Sarah book away until I had finished editing The Diary of Grief. But instead of finalising my selection from the accumulated mass of notes and journal entries, I found myself adding to it.

Alicja urged me to set myself a deadline for finishing the Diary. Almost thirty years after Sarah's death, I replied that I can't finish it yet because I haven't finished living it. After thirty years!

'Living it' meant still expecting to discover an ultimate satisfying revelation, finding hints of its whereabouts and chasing urgently after them. Only when I had found it would the book have an ending. But this attempt to define 'living it' is made years later. At the time, I was driven only by vague unexamined feelings of incompletion, urgency and hope.

I want DG to be truthful to my experience of the astonishing world of grief, for which I was as unprepared as I had been for the revelations of parenthood, and in which I have lived for nearly thirty years. I didn't set out to help others in grief or offer them advice; I would not be so presumptuous. I have tried to serve the reality that has forced itself on me, by bearing witness to that experience, and to the uneven and often baffling process of learning.

After compiling another list of absurd deaths, I came across a pertinent comment in an essay by John Bayley:
> Jane Austen … writes in a letter about a bloody battle in the Napoleonic war: 'How dreadful that so many poor fellows should be killed, and what a mercy that one cares for none of them.' There speaks the voice of a certain kind of common sense, the kind that most of us have to live by.

And I, how much do I care about those grotesque deaths? Probably no more than Jane Austen. I started collecting them soon after she died, to help convince myself that her sudden death, with its trivial-seeming cause and infinite consequences, is not an unprecedented outrage, but that deaths from sudden, unlikely, irrelevant and disproportionate causes are an everyday occurrence and one of the defining possibilities of human life. I still need reminders.

From time to time I look back over these years of grief, and try to distinguish its various concerns. I draw up schemes with headings and subheadings, of the aims of grief (*my* grief), or of its many contradictions, or of what has been mad and what sane in my searchings, or of the different needs served by my mottoes. Some of these schemes are elaborate, worked on enthusiastically, condensed into diagrams, typed and retyped, under the illusion that I am learning to master experience and clarify important truths. But each time, a day or so later, I am bored with my classification. It has lost its resonance and I don't refer to it again. If my taxonomies don't interest me, they won't interest anyone else, and I shan't include any of them here. 'Grey is all theory, green is life's golden tree.'

I read every personal story by a bereaved parent that I find. At the time of Sarah's death in 1964 few such stories had been published, and those early books said little about the aftermath of death, but usually focussed on the course of a tragic illness, and parental struggles with medical and other authorities. I have drawn from them a private anthology about the courage and realism of young children who know that they are dying. Since then, many heartfelt accounts about experiencing the death of a child have appeared, often published by small provincial presses, finding the audience that needs them but unnoticed by the general reading public. I am always moved while reading them, but the situations and responses of grief are repetitive, and I soon forget most of these elegies.

Two that I have not forgotten, that are unforgettable, but which are not otherwise referred to in these diaries are Blessings, *by Mary Craig, and* Will, My Son, *by Sarah Boston. Boston's later book,* Too Deep for Tears, *is the best discussion of long-term grief that I have found.*

An exception for me has been *Year One*, by John Tittensor, whose two children, Jonathan and Emma, died in a house fire at Belgrave, in the Dandenongs outside Melbourne. I have read and reread it and live with it still – because of Tittensor's perceptive and vivid writing, but also because his world is mine. We both come from Melbourne, we attended the same University, our thinking and reading overlap, the places in which he lived are familiar (I have known Belgrave since I was a child). he evokes the Australian setting of Sarah's last years of life and my first years of mourning. His experience is almost close enough to be mine, but it is not mine, and in some ways very different, yet I read with a sense of sharing, taking his life into mine and seeing mine in his.

His grief is wild and uninhibited: weeping and calling out his children's names into the silent bush, cries that seem to express the ferocity of my emotion in a way I never dared. But I recognise many of the contradictory reactions which he packed into one year ; I have asked the impossible questions he tries to answer – how we should honour the dead, how regain calm and vigour in living without being disloyal to them, how incorporate the knowledge of their love and of their deaths into our lives.

And sometimes a memory of Emma seems like a

memory of Sarah. He describes an extraordinary stretch of volcanic country outside Melbourne, where we once were with her.

> The first time I ever visited here, years ago, I had the kids with me and we climbed that steep rocky-grassy slope, abruptly finding ourselves in the wild emptiness of the plateau. Boulders, lichen, animal bones: all that stony ancientness, silence, suspension of time. And Emmy turning through a full circle to take it all in, her arms spread: 'It's like a new world!' she cried rapturously…

Emmy could be Sarah. I type out large chunks of *Year One*, which I borrowed from the library of The Compassionate Friends, but I can't buy a copy for myself because in the absurd lottery of present-day publishing it is out of print.

Some time later I talked to an Australian TCF member about John Tittensor's book. 'It's not much use,' she said. 'It doesn't offer any Consolation.' But there is no Consolation. There are alleviations, consolations with a small c, and one of them is to share and meditate on someone else's loss and grief. It is a way of exploring your own experience, of remembering that you are not the only one, of distancing your anguish and at the same time confirming its reality.

Later still, I did manage to buy a copy of Year One, *published by Penguin Books in Melbourne, with Daniel's help, via the internet and a bookseller in Portland, Oregon, an achievement that only those of my generation would find surprising.*

'She is dead and I am alive' – the final response to those qualms about enjoying my life when she has been robbed of hers. A simple lesson and one of the last to be recognised – I don't think I have ever stated it so baldly before, and even now I flinch. But I need to repeat it and I do, not as a cry of protest or a soothing incantation, but as a plain statement of reality. Nothing to be done for her; a duty and a desire to live for me.

Two days later: I have reread that last entry and see that I was wrong in thinking it a new refrain. I have said something similar many times. It is one of the truths that have to be constantly rediscovered, which each time seem a new revelation, and perhaps are never totally accepted.

Incomprehensibility. 'It is the hardest thing in the world to understand the difference between life and death,' *The Daniel Diary* records my telling three-year-old Daniel. Thirty years later I am still utterly bewildered when I think of her vivid presence suddenly obliterated by the darkness of death. Fleeting solace just now on finding this stupefaction put into words by someone else – by Edward Blishen in an interview with Rosemary Dinnage.

> I think for me, I would say, ultimately, the destruction of this elaborate individual life, with all its great experience, its longings, its hopes – the destruction of every human life is incomprehensible, ultimately incomprehensible. It's impossible really to understand.

Longings and hopes, but possibilities also – the power to create unimaginable acts of understanding and energy and love. And suddenly, in a fraction of a second, it has gone. I can understand why some people believe in an after-life. Julien Green, remembering the greatness of Colette, found it simply unthinkable that she should no longer exist.

I still haven't quite got rid of the yearning for a publicly accepted non-believer's ritual for the dead, despite recalling the florid absurdity of Robespierre's Festival of Reason, despite D.J.Enright's convincing dismissal of invented ritual in *The Oxford Book of Death*, and my rejection of such newly-designed ceremonies as I have read about or attended. But lately I have come to see merit in established religious ritual. It is not intrusive, like ceremonies newly designed for bereaved parents. One doesn't have to be moved; it is there for those who need it when they need it. The weight of time and custom confers dignity even when one feels uninvolved, or sceptical.

My actual sharing in any kind of ritual has been minimal, but I have welcomed an elusive Anglican prayer 'for those who are with us but on another shore'. I heard it on a rare occasion of attending church on Christmas Day, and thought of her with love and longing, and a wispy belief that she was indeed waiting for me on that distant shore. The evocation worked because it was impersonal. No-one expected me to think of her, or knew that I did so. But when I returned to the same church this Christmas, hoping to hear that prayer, I found that the traditional service had been abandoned for trendy audience-participation. So even ancient ritual can't be relied on.

'You can't spend your life in mourning,' Barbara Falk said all those years ago, when I told her that I was writing about Sarah. If to write about her is to mourn, then I *have* spent my life in mourning, nearly thirty years of it, during which Barbara's admonition has often risen up to judge me. But I defy it. To write about Sarah, about a young child, about death and grief, to write at all, is not simply to mourn. It is to undertake a long and varied course of thinking and reading and learning, and to acquire a competence, a profession and a commitment. This writing has felt necessary as no work before ever did. Writing about her and about grief became my way of coping with death – and with life. In the end I categorically deny that you can't. I can, I have, I had to, and it was right.

I have to use ill-fitting words; there are no others. Iris Murdoch: 'Is one then to be, for fear of lying, silent about such deep matters, as Wittgenstein sometimes recommended? Such silence is contrary to respectable human instincts, we must talk, it keeps things going.' And stopping to brood about etymology and divergent meanings doesn't help. In the end one just has to follow one's own instinctive taste. I always hated the phrase 'coming to terms', with its connotations of simplicity, commerce and contract (with whom?). It is widely used but I think I have avoided it. 'Acceptance' suggests willingness and satisfaction, and is almost as bad, but seems impossible to escape. Perhaps 'acknowledgment' is better.

And what of 'recovery', another word I met early on, and which at first I didn't question? 'She never fully recovered', a phrase encountered repeatedly in biographies, said something I wanted to hear. More recently I have felt astonished that those biographers of thirty or forty years ago could dismiss with this banal phrase the devastation caused by the early death of a child. But I too have used it. 'Have I recovered?' I have repeatedly asked myself. Two witty explorations of alternative clichés suggest that the answer cannot be simple.

C.S.Lewis:

> Getting over it so soon? But the words are ambiguous. To say the patient is getting over it after an operation for appendicitis is one thing; after he's had his leg off it is quite another. After that operation either the wounded stump heals or the man dies. If it heals, the fierce, continuous pain will stop. Presently he'll get back his strength and be able to stump about on his wooden leg. He has 'got over it'. But he will probably have recurrent pains in the stump all his life, and perhaps pretty bad ones; and he will always be a one-legged man...

and Julian Barnes:

> 'It may seem bad, Geoffrey, but you'll come out of it. I'm not taking your grief lightly; it's just that I've seen enough of life to know that you'll come out of it'... And you do come out of it, that's true. After a

year, after five. But you don't come out of it like a train coming out of a tunnel, bursting through the Downs into sunshine and that swift, rattling descent to the Channel; you come out of it as a gull comes out of an oil-slick. You are tarred and feathered for life.

A note written about three weeks ago: 'Still, after thirty years, she can appear before me, as she did this morning, a living centre of onward-surging strength, unconquerable and immortal – not in the next world but in this. That is what she was and must continue to be. I disbelieve in the possibility of her death even more than in my own. A mad faith that perhaps is essential to human endurance and optimism.'

Rereading these words today, I ask – 'What on earth is that supposed to mean? Consoling windy phrases like those I dismiss scornfully in others?' Recently I read to Alicja a sentence from Tittensor, moved by its apparent sincerity, but wondering how it was to be applied in reality: 'Everything I do for the rest of my life will be done in their name.' Alicja commented, 'Human beings seem to need these vague phrases.' Well I seem to need them too, despite my puritan views about plain speaking. They appear often enough in the original spontaneous versions of my various diaries, though I hope I have censored out most of them in this selection.

Alicja told me that the sixteenth-century Polish poet Jan Kochanowski began to write out of grief for the death of his daughter. Today, she rang to say she had seen a play about Kochanowski, in which an angel tells him that, because of his profound sorrow, his daughter can be returned to him – but the price will be the surrender of the only copy of his poems. Alicja did not say whether the play revealed his choice. I have absolutely no doubt that I would chose her, but I would lose the two books that I have written because of her death, and the self I have created through writing them. Who would I be then? Their joyful mother – Daniel's also, because he would be again the confident cheerful lieutenant he was in her lifetime. But who else? Impossible to know whether I would ever have emerged from domesticity to achieve any other 'doing'.

'She would fix her great brown eyes on someone with a look of such grave compassion that I was convinced she knew and understood everything.' This was one of the first sentences I wrote after Sarah died. I tried hard to find a place for it in the book about her, but finally saw that it did not belong there, since it tells more about me than about her, and more about grief than about childhood. It is true that sometimes her expression seemed to convey great wisdom; friends commented on it. But the memory of that serious watchful look grew into the passionate delusion that death had not cheated her of any essential human understanding. I wanted to believe that in her five years she had experienced the whole of life.

I still believe she saw more than we commonly imagine so young a child sees, and was storing up impressions that would have helped her later to understand herself and other people, but I am finally able to admit that she did not possess the wisdom of some serene ancient who has known and forgiven all.

My morning shower fosters contemplation and ideas come to me there – 'shower thoughts'. Today's shower thought: I have spent years meditating on what it means to die at five years old, and suddenly I seem to have no inkling of what it means to meditate on what it means. Her death is simply a plain brute fact with no meaning beyond that. I can't imagine how I could have spent nearly thirty years trying to understand it. But clearly I am still doing so. This book is a distillation of that meditation – and if I don't know what it is about at least I know I'm swamped with material.

'I leave her behind in the past, I recognise more often that there is nothing I can do for her, she fades into the distance, I lose the sense of an obligation of loyalty.' That is what I found myself writing this morning, after almost thirty years! Again! How many times previously have I discovered this sad necessity? Because it is a matter of degree, of stops and starts, of a slow almost imperceptible change that is never absolute. Like the growth of understanding, like abandoning the conviction of privileged immunity, like acknowledging one's own mortality.

I watched a TV programme about *The Wizard of Oz*, which, I learn, has been an essential book for more writers than I would have guessed. Salman Rushdie, looking older, heavier, sleeker, wiser, commented that the story's moral for children is that their parents cannot give them everything they need. And for parents the moral is the same from a different perspective – we cannot give our children everything we long to give, or that they need to receive from us. I've experienced this lesson often enough in relation to Daniel. Suddenly I applied it with new clarity to Sarah's death.

I made two chastening discoveries while writing the Sarah book: that in her lifetime I had floated on an illusion of omnipotence; and that on her last day my own uncomprehending actions and failures to act had been part of the pattern of events that carried her to death. The first seems a forgivable absurdity, the second has carried intermittent guilt, yes, even though I know it is impossible to say what would have happened had any of us acted differently. But Rushdie implied that parental failure is universal and almost impersonal, a consequence of human limitations and of the structure of the world. So I come to see my failure to save her as beyond my powers, a cause for sorrow but not for guilt.

It is not true that our culture lacks help or support in grief to those outside the established religions, and outside the grief-counselling industry, which hardly existed when Sarah died, and with which I have had no dealings, except through The Compassionate Friends. Support is there and essential, but it isn't concentrated in one place waiting to be picked up, but must be accumulated slowly, in fragments, a different collection for each person. If I have recovered, it is with the help of a great many writers, living and dead – many more than I can acknowledge here. I have survived through words, an infinity of words. Though I could not easily summarise what they have told me.

I often recall a remark by Erich Heller. Commenting on the frequently-held view that the sincerity of the poet is irrelevant to the value of a poem, he suggests that, on the contrary, some poems evidently express deeply held convictions, and that 'the *aesthetic* success of this kind of poetry is inextricably bound up with the sincerity of the personal beliefs expressed in them.' But, he goes on to say, whether the poet remains a believer all the time, when he is not writing poetry, and whether he realises his beliefs in his actions. are other matters. 'Few men are like Pascal, and even he had to remind himself continually, by a sheet of paper sewn into his jacket, of what he had on one sacred occasion recognised as wholly true.' I often forget what I have learned, and must remind myself by repeating or rediscovering one or other of my collection of texts. Like Pascal!

It is a commonplace that a deeply felt death forces us to contemplate our own mortality. It was not so for me. I didn't start thinking about the inevitability and nearness of my own death until quite recently – until I was getting to the end of writing about her death, and until, at about the same time, the symptoms of relentless aging became increasingly obvious. Nowadays I note that there's not all that much time left for me; I try to imagine non-existence; I remind myself that accident or fatal illness can befall me at any moment; but all without terror or other sharp emotion, without a full sense of reality. Her death is still *the* death, Death itself, the incomprehensible mystery, the revelation by which I try to understand other deaths and other griefs.

I have never turned to music for consolation. Not to the great requiems, not to the Beethoven quartets, not to the *Kindertotenlieder*. I positively avoid them, and if by chance I hear death-music, I listen detachedly, not thinking of her. The one piece which occasionally intrudes on me by speaking of her death is Schubert's *Erlkönig*, but I push it away. My first interpretation of this reluctance was that music evokes emotions of sorrow and inevitability too powerfully. But music also conveys acceptance. Must it be? It must be! Well I don't want to hear it that way. I am basically a word person. Words are what I want.

The multifarious shapes of denial! That stubborn conviction that she understood and experienced everything! As late as l987 I asked in a journal entry, 'Did she have a fulfilled life?' Absurd question! She fulfilled the possibilities of a five-year-old, and not those that would open up with growing experience, intelligence, independence. And which are more various, and more challenging? Certainly more interesting to most people. All this is obvious and the only thing I demonstrate by recording it as a discovery is the myopia of grief. But a tribute of Cecily's is too impersonal to warm my heart – 'She fulfilled each stage so beautifully.' I don't want to think of her as an example of stages in development, however beautiful. I don't want to sum up her life in a phrase but to remember her as she was at different moments of a complex past. But then I do sometimes try to sum her up in a few words – joy, exuberance, love. And in addition to particular memories which return unbidden, I have, constantly, a wordless sense of her vivid presence, which is a sort of summary.

I am reading *Beckett's Dying Words*, by Christopher Ricks. Here is someone who speaks a language I can accept. He begins with a masterly survey of literary attitudes to death, whose tone is different from anything else I have read – concise, witty, involved but unappalled, commonsensical, totally devoid of those familiar clerical cooings. And he has a fund of apt quotations, mostly new to me even when he calls them well-known, such as 'La

Rochefoucauld's famous apophthegm: 'Comme le soleil, la mort ne peut être regardée fixement,' whose implications he draws out with subtlety. I would like to memorise the whole of Ricks's first chapter. What has stuck most firmly in my memory is his brisk dismissal of that equivocal ideal 'acceptance':

> Nineteenth-century hopefulness set itself to accept the universe, including, reluctantly, its entropy. Twentieth-century hopefulness, to accept death? But acceptance could never be quite it. If our own imminent death is the issue, acceptance asks too much of us; if the fact of general mortality is the issue, acceptance is too grudging. For life would be unimaginably worse if we had to imagine it without death…

Highly original common sense! Though I make a familiar complaint – nothing said about the real impossibility – accepting the death of a dearly-loved other, of the most closely identified, of a child. His jokes about various public pronouncements on death are marvellously astringent. Beckett's also, and I am grateful to Ricks for pointing them out.

Julian Barnes's *Flaubert's Parrot* contains a wonderful list of disgusted comments on life taken (perhaps) from Flaubert's writings. For example:

> 1852 What an awful thing life is, isn't it? It's like soup with lots of hairs floating on the surface. You have to eat it nevertheless.

I laugh out loud. As I do at the story of Samuel Beckett walking across Hyde Park on a spring morning and remarking on its freshness and beauty. 'Yes, it makes you glad to be alive!' said his companion. Beckett: 'Well, I wouldn't go as far as that!' A story with the makings of myth. I remember reading this version though I don't recall where, but a recent biography of Beckett sites it at Lords Cricket Ground on a sunny summer afternoon.

Such remarks certainly belong in my scriptures. I don't reject life, despite her death. I am glad to be alive, and relish the intensity of the passing moment more as I see my own end approaching. But wry deprecation is the necessary counterpart to the elation that (perhaps, sometimes) accompanies an acceptance of death. Two extreme ultimate attitudes. I don't fully accept either, but I acknowledge that both are contained in that inconstant muddle which is my attitude to life.

In Paris, on my way to Majorca, I found on a table in the bookshop La Procure a vast series, or, rather a series of series, published by Editions Autrement, of volumes half-way between periodical and book, each a collection of essays by a number of authors on some contemporary topic. The titles ranged through topography, science, philosophy, sociology, morals, and daily life. I thought that if there were issues on Sleep, Being Old, Humour, The Obsession with Security, Single Parents, and Gluttony, there must be one on mourning, and after a search I found it – *Deuils,* a word for which English needs three, bereavement, grief and mourning, and often none provides a satisfactory translation.

Now in Majorca I have became totally absorbed in *Deuils*, reading, brooding, summarising articles, disputing, writing commentaries. The authors are philosophers, historians, sociologists, journalists, teachers, and yes, psychoanalysts, and their contributions have the qualities I welcomed in Christopher Ricks – intelligent, learned and literary, implicitly atheist, but not, like those books by psychotherapists, written from outside, *de haut en bas*. Instead, there is a sense of shared human involvement in the mystery of death and the pain of grief.

Most of the contributors assume that mourning can and should come to an end, which they define in various ways. For Julia Kristeva it is the arrival, not at indifference, but at serene memory; for Cecile Wajsbrot, the acknowledgement of 'Never more' ; for 'Alice', the ability to talk about the dead with humour, sadness, and above all with truth; and, from the keynote essay by the philosopher André Comte-Sponville, 'being able to say *Yes* to everything, and yes in particular to that *No* which, a few months or a few years earlier, lacerated our soul'.

Comte-Sponville inspired in me an exhilarating eagerness for the heroic task of learning to say Yes to every bitter reality, including her death at five. Which intermittently I retained for some years, despite starting to question the necessity and meaning of saying Yes.

Several of the *Deuils* writers point out that not much can be said about *how* one moves from the shock and pain of loss to the consummation of acceptance, other than that it takes a long time. I like that. There is no recipe, says Comte-Sponville; everyone just has to manage as best he can. 'To get over the death of La Boétie, Montaigne needed to write the *Essays,* no less.' This sentence immediately entered my repertoire. But did Montaigne need to write the *whole* of the Essays before his grief was assuaged? Has anyone searched the text for clues? I doubt it, and admire the sympathetic recklessness of Comte-Sponville's assertion.

In *Deuils* I found a remark by Francis, whose son Jean-Fred was killed a year earlier, at the age of twenty-two, in an explosion at his block of flats:
> Ce qui me fait du bien c'est qu'il y a quatre ans j'ai perdu une belle-soeur. J'ai dit à mon fils: 'C'est quand même malheureux de perdre la vie à trente-neuf ans.' Et il m'a répondu: 'Mais ça vaut le coup quand même.' Je m'accroche à des phrases comme ça.
>
> One thing that helps is that four years ago I lost a sister-in-law. I said to my son, 'Its pretty miserable to lose your life at thirty-nine.' And he replied, 'All the same, it's worth it.' I cling to phrases like that.

And I welcome this admission of the need to cling to phrases.

How are memories transformed from a source of anguish

and protest into that 'serene memory' which Julia Kristeva sees as the true end of mourning. Freud seems to suggest that this happens through one single recall. Writing the book about Sarah was a long and profound revisiting of memories. Finishing it brought a sense of rejoicing in her life, and of having reached an ending, but it didn't last. Anguish and revolt returned. I try to look back at occasions of remembering her, but my memories of memory have vanished. However I vividly recall a somewhat different experience, that of revisiting a site of hallowed memory.

I had planned to drive to Barcelona, en route for Majorca to join Daniel for Christmas. December was cold and snowy and I kept postponing my departure, but finally, one louring midday, I set off for Dover and caught a late-afternoon ferry. It started to snow while I was driving through the dark towards Montreuil, where I planned to spend the night, and by the time I had finished dinner, snow lay thick and immaculate on the deserted streets and ramparts of the old town. Next morning I drove in sparkling winter sunshine over near-empty roads, stopping for a short walk in the snow-filled park of Versailles. The transformed world was exhilarating for one who, in an Australian childhood, had never seen snow.

By the time I reached Tours and decided to stop again for the night, the snow had been left behind, but so had my euphoria. I normally avoid the impersonality of large towns when travelling alone, and the hotel was vast and drab. Tours was also a town of sacred memory, which I had visited thirty years earlier with Erwin and two-year-old Sarah, in the heady years of early parenthood. I avoid such places with a sense of terror, imagining that the three of us are still there, enclosed in an aura of blessedness, and dreading to shatter the illusion.

But there I was in Tours. Summoning up courage, I found my way after dinner to a street where we had walked together, in a part of town that had escaped wartime destruction and still kept an archaic provincial charm. I could not see into the garden where Sarah had been befriended by a small black girl, but the bookshop where I had bought her first bedtime book, *Les Animaux*, with large handsome pictures and minuscule text, was unchanged. I stood in the doorway, half imagining I could see the very book displayed in the window, and felt quietly thankful for past happiness. In that mood I think of Tours now. Memory has changed its quality.

People talk of acceptance as something absolute. 'I have accepted.' But I don't think anyone totally accepts either the inevitability of their own death or the reality of a beloved other's. There are times of fervent renunciation, but there continue also to be waverings, protests, the return of sharp despair, new perceptions. And forgettings, and movings on to other things. Even Comte-Sponville has reservations. 'Mourning is complete, *if ever it can be totally*, when we can say *yes* to everything…' And again, after pleading eloquently that we must learn to renounce, and to love in full awareness of the inevitability of loss:

> J'écris cela en tremblant, me sachant incapable d'une telle sagesse, mais convaincu pourtant (ou a cause de cela) qu'il n'y en a pas d'autre, si tant est qu'il y ait une, et que tel est à peu près le chemin sur lequel, ou vers lequel, et difficilement toujours, il nous faut avancer...
>
> I write this hesitatingly, knowing myself incapable of such wisdom, but convinced nevertheless (or for that very reason) that there is no other, if there is any at all, and that such is, more or less, the road along which, or towards which, and always uncertainly, we must go forward...

Dear Professor André Comte-Sponville, I am glad to have encountered both your fervour and your doubts.

To celebrate their first twenty-five years, the association of bereaved parents, The Compassionate Friends, has just held an International Gathering in Birmingham. I have subscribed to their newsletter for several years, and borrowed from their library, but although I have never attended a meeting, when the Gathering was announced, I decided to go. I hoped to meet people with similar literary and theoretical interests to mine. In the event, the reward wasn't exactly that. Then by the time I drove up to Birmingham two weeks ago I was worried about mawkishness and boredom. I didn't find those either.

It was a moving and thoroughly enjoyable occasion, attended by five hundred people who had in common not just an interest, but a profound life-changing experience.

That made a strong and unexpected bond. I talked to a continuous succession of people, easily and intimately, of matters I normally shut up about, from fear of embarrassment or pity or imputations of making too much fuss, and I listened with deep feeling to their stories. Although the bereavement of a few was recent and raw, for the majority of those attending their loss happened some time ago. We could talk calmly and enquiringly, and we needed to, since ordinary life rarely offers such opportunities. The phrase 'You are not the only one' acquired a different density.

I didn't feel particularly touched by the symbols and ceremonies devised for the occasion, which seemed forced, and too frail to bear the weight of my longing. But then it has been obvious for a long time that my desire for a satisfying modern ritual is a mirage. The service in Coventry Cathedral left me feeling merely exhausted – and mildly affronted that believers of every creed were explicitly welcomed, but non-believers not. Instead of moving from the new cathedral to the bombed ruins of the old, where the service was continued, I escaped in my car to a National Trust property, Baddesley Clinton, where I ate a huge recuperative afternoon tea and lingered in the romantic and beautiful gardens. That afternoon apart, the conference brought the experience of losing a child into the world of other people in a way that was both emotional and matter of fact.

Poetry of Mourning: The Modern Elegy from Hardy to

Heaney by Jahan Ramazani is the third (after *Beckett's Dying Words* and *Deuils*) of a trio of eminently sane books about death that I have come across recently. I read an appreciative review and then miraculously found it in the Kensington Public Library. I say miraculously because Dillons told me that they had only one copy on order. Which I now possess, though with guilt at monopolising it.

Ramazani, as if in answer to Comte-Sponville, distinguishes two modes of mourning: the normative (restitutive, idealizing, consolatory) and the melancholic (violent and recalcitrant.) Where the traditional elegy (and official psychoanalytic theory), has been normative and consolatory, the modern elegist (and Freud's private opinion in the letter to Dr Binswanger which I have long known and which Ramazani quotes) is unresolved, angry and scornful of recovery and transcendence, refusing both to let go of the dead and to heal the living. And absolutely right too, I thought. Without for that rejecting the teaching of Comte-Sponville.

So I return to the conclusion reached more than once in the diary, that I will continue to oscillate between acceptance and protest, serenity and anguish, gratitude for her life, and undiminished pain at her death. And most of the time now, perhaps, carry on with my daily concerns in a state of reasonableness where the knowledge of her death 'finds its place as part of a whole life rather than as something which dominates and distorts that life' – Tittensor's phrase, and as good as any other.

I collect pronouncements about writing, too. I need them as much as I need sayings about death. I have kept an interview with V. S. Naipaul from *The Sunday Times,* 10 November 1968.

> A man writing his first book sits down and pretends he's writing a book; that element is still with me. In fact it lasts for longer and longer with each book, until the moment you realise a book is there. It doesn't spring, it has to be called up, a sort of slow magic. You have to pretend to be writing a book until you discover who you are.

As true for a struggling amateur as for a brilliant professional. I have thought of it while attempting to transform this mass of diary notes into a book to be called, perhaps, A Necessary Madness. A long stage of pretence, and before that, a time when I wasn't even pretending to write a book – just tentatively surveying, examining problems, hoping, doubting. I once drew up a page-long list of reasons why this book was impossible. And now, slowly, something that seems like a book, is coming into being.

I heard Dame Edith Evans on the radio, reading, superbly, Shakespeare's lyric:

> Golden lads and girls all must,
> As chimney sweepers, come to dust.

A reminder – or a lesson – that what has to be accepted is not simply death, including the hardest of all, her death. I have worked doggedly at that – remembering, repeating slogans, reading theories, trying to stare fixedly at it. And I've remembered her life too, writing a book about it, recalling it in joyful flashes. But what needs to be accepted, what requires that Yes, is the two simultaneously, golden girls and dusty death. It's a more heart-raising prospect than the dour effort merely 'to say Yes to that No which has lacerated our soul.' For a little while this morning I seem to succeed. I hold in mind both her living image, fresh as a rose in June, and the desolation of her death. I feel exalted and breathless, close to the ultimate mystery.

I have fallen out of grief, as one falls out of love, suddenly bored with it all, not wanting to question my emotions or to write about them, no longer fascinated. All that exhilaration and intensity has gone. Grief still returns, just as love may survive after one 'falls out of love', and I feel it acutely for a few minutes, but I'm not 'in' grief any more.

And did I fall into grief as I might have fallen in love? Not immediately, but when the first numbness wore off, yes, I was plunged into a state in which her death was the only thing that mattered in the entire world, and thinking about it the only preoccupation that was worthwhile or even possible. Total absorption in grieving, as in the first days of falling in love. And then for a long time an intense but fluctuating involvement which persisted alongside other revived desires. And now seems to have evaporated completely.

IX

Afterwords
2000 – Infinity

That looked like an ending. I finished editing a selection of diary entries, and tried it out on a few readers, personal and professional, receiving, in turn, mild praise, flattering enthusiasm and salutary criticism. Then I put the diaries away and left for Australia on my first visit for 25 years, in a spirit of triumphant release from grief and from the self-imposed duty of writing about it. Daniel was living in Sydney with Ingrid, whom he would later marry. It was the first new optimistic love that had appeared in our family for a long time. I spent several carefree months, happy in the company of Dan and Ingrid, discovering Sydney, and revisiting the trees of home.

When I took up the diary again, several years later, I found that there had indeed been an ending. I was no longer driven by the urgent hope of finding, perhaps in the very book I was about to read, some magisterial and final revelation. The obsession I called 'the search for the Grail' had vanished. But on rereading the 1966 version of the Diary of Grief, I found there was more I wanted to say. I looked afresh at past discoveries, and new books appeared that I found sympathetic or enlightening or provocative.

What did I hope to find in those years of 'searching for the Grail'? I seldom used to ask. Now it seems like a search with no goal – or a hundred. A search for nothing, like the questionings of Rush Rhees's bereaved mother, but a search that was nevertheless worthwhile. A necessary madness. If I did not find the Grail, I made discoveries, compiled a scriptures of my own, learned a great deal about the sufferings and reactions of others, and gained a better understanding of reality and wider and more ready sympathies.

Underneath all that, I can see two aims. I was trying to keep her alive – to resurrect her, give birth to her again, sustain a belief that she never really died, save from oblivion something of her essential being, live still in close communion with her. And I was trying to reconcile myself to her death and to the world in which her life could be capriciously destroyed. Two passionate endeavours, each taking many shapes, pulling in opposite directions, and both impossible of fulfilment. No wonder it has gone on for so long.

Occasionally I question, aghast, whether it has been wasted effort, and I would have reached the same state of relative calm simply through the passing of time. I don't really believe it, but I couldn't say how my present state differs from what it might have been had I just abandoned her to time and forgetfulness. Yet there has been an intensity in this psychological-philosophical-moral quest which I would not have missed. It is, as much as anything, part of the 'meaning of life'.

'Burying her in new experience', – a rueful discovery of the early days. It was a long time before I saw that from the first moment we were also burying her in familiar experience, by simply getting on with the ordinary domestic routines in which she no longer had a place, starting with the first cup of tea on the first morning. Creating a daily life without her. It is the fundamental process of recovery. Not consoling, just sobering and distancing.

'The return to normality has to be at the cost of the recession of the lost one… If the mutilated personality is to survive, it cannot be by trying to keep the Other alive.' I have often recalled these words of Mary Stott, from *Forgetting's No Excuse*, her memoir about surviving the death of her husband. They seem to express a basic truth. Others have said the same, including Freud – libido must be withdrawn from the lost love object. And yet I don't quite agree. They are true, but also not true. Some of my ways of keeping her alive, especially that of writing about her, were themselves a return to normality.

I want to add that I haven't stopped loving her. But I begin to reflect on the differences between loving the living and loving the dead, differences which we ignore in our passionate denials that we will ever stop loving. One can have more than one love, and when the first all-else-obliterating desolation has waned, attachment to the dead need not be at the expense of the living. But it is different, one-sided. One has to do all the work oneself. The lost love may be 'loved deeplier, darklier understood' –

although, in thinking about her lost life, I didn't so much discover new truths as see mysteries where before I had assumed understanding – but she can't add anything new to the relationship. Love no longer changes as the events of life are shared. What remains is composed of memory, longing and the tenderness one feels for the vulnerable. (Who more vulnerable than the helpless dead?) Well, infinite differences – obvious but easily forgotten.

And sometimes I think that love for the dead is an easy option. The dead don't surprise, disappoint, betray or desert. Just the thing for an aging woman who has few present loves and who has known real desertions.

> Every book has an intrinsic impossibility, which its writer discovers as soon as his first excitement dwindles. The problem is structural; it is insoluble; it is why no one can ever write this book. (Annie Dillard, *The Writing Life*)

I discovered the impossibility of this book early. My material is repetitive, private, monotonous, abstract; there are (almost) no events, characters or settings; it lacks climax and resolution. An impossible book. It is bleak comfort to learn from Annie Dillard that all books are impossible. She doesn't suggest giving up on that account. The writer, she says, writes in spite of that.

> ... And if it can be done, then he can do it, and only he. For there is nothing in the material for this book that suggests to anyone but him alone its possibilities for meaning and feeling.

AFTERWORDS

I don't imagine that no-one else will ever see the possibilities of this book, nor that only I can write it, but no-one else to my knowledge has yet done so. And it is needed, whether or not I can write it. A book, that is, which explores the realities confronting, and the consolations offering themselves to, the bereft non-believer. So I plug on. But not just for that reason. Because I want to see the overflowing untidy mass of typed pages and computer files reduced to neatness and surveyability. And because I have committed myself to it. I want to finish the job.

Alconasser. A morning working at the computer, assailed by familiar doubts as I reread early journal entries. I break off, to sit on the terrace with a cup of coffee, watching the sea change from leaden grey to serene grey-blue as a threatened storm passes over. In an old copy of the *New York Review of Books*, I read a demand by Adam Zagajewski for more histories written from the viewpoint of the participating 'sovereign individual' – a category in which he includes diaries and autobiographies.

I'm not writing any history but my own, but Zagajewski's words seem to justify what I am doing. Suddenly I feel a fierce exultation in being my individual self, free to write what I want to write, without regard to whether others will find it interesting or the right thing to have done. Exultation too in my good fortune at being in this calm beautiful place, with history-soaked France and Spain so near, to be visited on my way home. A sense of self-containment, even while I am gratefully aware of the family in Sydney and the coming baby, my second grandchild.

I have at last found another collector of maxims. In a beguiling essay in *Etre Vieux*, a companion volume to *Deuils,* Georges Mounin, octogenarian teacher and writer, describes what he calls the 'rampart of twigs' which he has built as a defence against the trials and terrors of old age. 'For a long while,' he writes, 'my antidote has been prolonged meditation on well-expressed fragments of experience encountered through chance reading.' He lists some forty sayings, most of them very short. Examples:
  'Old age, you have arrived.' Saint-John Perse
  'Am I really as old as I know I am?' Umberto Saba
  'Growing old is hard, but no-one has found any other way of living for a long time.' Alexander Dumas
  'It is already late, but there is still time.' Jean Malrieu
Our common habit gives me a sense of fellowship with Georges Mounin, but few of his sayings resonate for me. Because they come to me without the contexts of life and literature in which he found them; because aphorisms must be meditated singly, and lists are always deadening; because I haven't shared his meditations, since I feel the indignities of age less sharply than the never-healing wound of her death; and perhaps above all because the recognition that a particular sequence of words possesses a magic power

to teach, invigorate and sustain is an unpredictable personal experience.

Most anthologies of sorrow and mourning are too anxious to console, and hence full of patent falsities. I have found only three that I value – Enright's *Oxford Book of Death*, *A Book of Consolations* by P. J. Kavanagh, and Iris Origo's *The Vagabond Path*. But their choices, those that are relevant for me, are not enough. I don't want elegant restraint, I want a huge mass of words, a vast chorus of truth-telling.

Which I am assembling for myself in my files of Quotes on the computer. There, ranged under broad headings, I have an anthology copious enough to satisfy me, easily available when I want to verify words or meanings, and when I need reassurance or consolation or a dose of clearheadedness, or amusement, or mental stimulation, or renewed exultation at the originality and subtlety of human minds and human words. It is a manual of spiritual guidance, with the help of which I can restore the sense of being fully and deeply alive, can rejoice in blessings and more nearly accept what cannot be accepted. Each time I look up a half-remembered quotation, I read another four or five that I have forgotten; and in a melancholy or meditative or just an idle mood, I can browse at random and make surprising and often exhilarating rediscoveries. It is my scriptures in this age of individualism.

In the library I pick up a collection of essays on *The Humanist View of Life*, and turn to the one on 'The Meaning of Death'. The author, a scientist, distinguishes between natural death and untimely death, and devotes the rest of his article to an enthusiastic celebration of natural death. Not a word more about untimely death and what can be said about that.

I think more often now of how little of life is left for *me*. And in the *The Poem Itself,* a duplicate copy of which I found in a secondhand bookshop in Sydney and bought as a rarity, I read Hölderlin: 'If once I have achieved the sacred goal, my heart's desire, the poem, then welcome, silence of the shadow world! I am content …'

And will I have achieved my own sacred aim? It will not be what I vaguely imagined when I was young, some brilliant piece of academic reseach. Like Caitlin Thomas, 'I was under the quaint misapprehension that I was unique, specially chosen to fulfil a great, if somewhat ambiguous mission.' But this morning I accept that my three books (supposing I finish this third) are an achievement in the measure of my gifts, not brilliant, but a true record of experience and the best I can do. I am thankful for the two that are finished, A Shining Space and *The Daniel Diary*.

And does Erwin echo Hölderlin? Telling me of an invitation to attend a memorial gathering and dinner for Fred Gruen, thanks to having painted a portrait of him more than fifty years ago, he said wryly, 'That's what I'm famous for.' The achievement of his recent sculpture is far too seldom acknowledged. But then he often says that all he cares about is working at it, and sometimes he is pleased with the result. I hope that occasionally he too can say 'Zufrieden bin ich.'

I have meditated recently on the phrase *'en pure perte'*, encountered in André Comte-Sponville's essay in *Deuils*. 'We must always love *en pure perte;* ... wanting to keep is already to lose; death can only deprive us of what we try to possess.'

For Comte-Sponville, *en pure perte* is a powerful phrase to which my dictionaries don't do justice. *Cassell's French Dictionary* says 'to no purpose, uselessly, in vain'. *Robert* gives 'inutilement, sans aucun profit'. It can be used in very humdrum contexts. Comte-Sponville gives it a stronger meaning, which emphasizes the immensity of the reward we must forgo. We must learn to love in the certainty of absolute loss, without the assurance of eternal, or long-lasting, or even tomorrow's happiness. Sometimes I get near to it. Recently I spent three superb autumn days in Venice with Erwin, who was about to return to Australia for at least a year. I relished everything, sun and air and water and splendid buildings, and being together, with a sort of exultation in the pure present, without fear or envy. As I get older, such moments of love *en pure perte*, often for very ordinary experiences, come more frequently (although they are still rare).

But how do you love *en pure perte* a love already lost?

By loving what *was*, without the obscuring anguish of loss. Immensely difficult. I achieved it a times while writing A Shining Space, and again when I reread certain of its pages. And sometimes now, when a memory of her comes unexpectedly. *En pure perte* is a variant of the lines of Blake which I long ago took as a motto:
> He who binds to himself a joy
> Does the winged life destroy;
> But he who kisses the joy as it flies
> Lives in eternity's sunrise.

Adopting other people's words is clutching at authority. Not the monolithic authority of an established church, but the piecemeal authority of individual writers. But which writers does one choose as authorities?

Sixty years ago, as an undergraduate at Melbourne University, I heard a subversive intervention by Dan Taylor, Lecturer in Philosophy, at the lunchtime meeting of some religious society. He argued that it is not because we recognise his moral authority as the Son of God that we accept the teachings of Jesus; on the contrary, we acknowledge his moral authority because we recognise the rightness of his teachings. Have I then singled out my philosophers and sages because they say what I already believe? Almost always, to some degree, yes. They say memorably what I have thought but not so well expressed, or, more often, what I almost thought but couldn't put into words, or what appealed to my temperament and way of thinking. Nearly always there is some element of choosing authorities who teach what I already know or half know, or dimly suspect.

Iris Murdoch wants us to 'take in our mortality and see the world in its light.' I adapt her words to make them my own. Something like that is what I have been trying to do, intermittently and fumblingly. To take in her mortality and to see it in the light of how the world is.

Still hankering after a new ritual, I picture a scene in which we staunch unbelievers repeat together some assertion of courage in the face of cosmic indifference and the impossible fate of our children. What immediately springs to mind is W.E. Henley's boast:
> In the fell clutch of circumstance
> I have not winced nor cried aloud.
> Under the bludgeonings of chance
> My head is bloody but unbow'd.

Well no, not that! And we have all done a lot of wincing and crying aloud. Did Henley write it before or after the death of his own daughter?

> Other people's mourning – like other people's sexuality and other people's religions – is something one has to have a special reason to be interested in. So to write a book, as Leon Wieseltier has done, about the mourning of his father is asking a lot

(and to write a book of 585 pages is asking even more.)

 Adam Phillips, reviewing *Kaddish*, by Leon Wieseltier.

It is a perennial objection, the classic example being Edward Fitzgerald's complaint about Tennyson:

> We have surely had enough of men reporting their sorrows: especially when one is aware all the time that the poet wilfully protracts what he complains of, magnifies it in the Imagination, puts it into all the shapes of Fancy: and yet we are to condole with him, and be taught to ruminate our losses and sorrows in the same way. I felt that if Tennyson had got on a horse and ridden 20 miles, instead of moaning over his pipe, he would have been cured of his sorrows in half the time.

But people *are* interested, and I promptly got hold of Wieseltier's book. Most of its 585 pages are not in fact about personal mourning at all. Having decided to observe the Jewish tradition of saying kaddish for his father, Wieseltier not only attended shul twice a day for a year, but became obsessed by the history of kaddish, and writes at length at about his researches into medieval commentaries – much more than I want to know.

 Wieseltier says that by living with kaddish he is also living with his father, but he says little about his father or about his feelings at his father's death. He is no soul-barer or wailer and moaner (and I no longer have much patience with public wailing and moaning), but scattered through the book are snatches of autobiography and a few deft remarks about grief and mourning. He comments, for example, on Ecclesiastes, that its truth is not the whole truth:

> For the preacher, death is oblivion. For the mourner, death is not oblivion… A man dies with the death of his body, but his death is almost never complete. He survives himself in many ways, he leaves many traces of himself behind, in his work and in the people he loved. Whether or not the soul has immortality, then, the soul has posterity. The preacher erred in overlooking this distinction.

She survives in the people she loved and who loved her, and in the images and gestures she left with them. And the central task I set myself after the funeral was to preserve and extend that posterity.

How do I know what I think until I see what I write? But also, how do I know what I think until I read what someone else has written? Just now, it is Isaiah Berlin's slant on non-belief that I adopt as my own:

> … ever since I persuaded myself that a personal God – an old man with a beard – the Ancient of Days – or anyway some kind of individual conceivable in human terms – was unlikely to exist, I have never known the meaning of the word God; and I cannot even claim to be an atheist or an agnostic – I am somewhat like a tone-deaf person in relation to music…

The attainment of serene memory – Julia Kristeva's definition of the end of mourning. It has taken me a long time to get there. Until recently, whenever a joyful scene from her life flashed before my mind, it triggered an anguished protest at her early death. Happy memories sharpened the pain of loss. Only in the last few years has memory become a simple blessing.

There is a village in France whose name I don't recall, where we once spent the night, in an ancient room with a sloping floor, and a window opening onto a vast sweep of wooded countryside glowing in the early morning light with varied blues and greens, and she there with us, waking to the happiness of a new day. Later she sat between us as we drove through a world transformed to shining crystal by enormous hailstones which covered the ground like snow. Doubtless she did not share our surprise and enthralment, but the beauty of that glittering whiteness and the joy of her presence mutually heightened the sense of blessing. I could identify the place by tracing our itinerary, but I prefer to think of it as a fragment of eternal paradise, existing somewhere beyond mundane reality.

Recently I made an unplanned return to another place of blessed memory, a village on the river Tarn where we spent a night when she was two. The river is crossed by a narrow bridge with decorative iron railings that have survived from an earlier age. In the dusk of that late August evening, no cars went by as the landlord escorted us across to our room in an annexe on the far side. A dog ran out in front of us. 'Ya-ya!' Sarah called out excitedly.

'She calls dogs ya-ya,' I told the patron, proud that she had invented her own word instead of using the conventional bow-wow. 'That's what all children say,' he replied in a bored tone. Stupid unappreciative man I thought. I've never heard a French child say 'ya-ya'.

Now, on this sunny July morning, there are still no cars on the bridge, but groups of serious walkers are setting out to climb the *causses*, holiday-makers gaze down at the swirling water, and Sarah, on the deserted bridge, between the elegant iron railings, leans forward in her pushchair, joyfully calling out 'Ya-ya!' With pleasure untainted by grief, I rejoice in serene memory.

Survivors of trauma often say things like 'I am stronger, I have come closer to reality, I have learned what is important and what is not.' I can't make those claims. They are too absolute. When people say to me, 'It must have made you stronger,' I am disconcerted and more inclined to deny than to agree. One forgets what one was like before, as Cecily once said to me apropos the impossibility of assessing what psychoanalysis had done for her.

Inga Clendinnen, at the end of *Tiger's Eye*, a book which both reports and transcends the story of an appalling near-mortal illness, comments that she finds herself 'battered, possibly wiser, certainly wearier, and oddly happier.' I admire the modesty, economy and tentativeness of her summary, and would like to borrow at least two of her phrases. Possibly wiser. And, now, oddly happier than in most of the years since her death. There were long periods when I used to tell myself, 'You don't have to be happy. You just have to keep going.' I no longer need that injunction.

Recalling that first comforting chant, 'Keep right on to the end of the road,' I look it up on the internet. I find that the song is still well-known, has some 19 million Google entries, has been adopted by the Birmingham Football Club as its anthem, and was written by Sir Harry Lauder after his son was killed in action in the First World War. The last fact confirms the appropriateness of my choice, but I am glad I didn't have the rest of the information at the time. I liked to imagine that I was making a unique personal choice.

Thinking about my fervent 'search for the Grail', it strikes me now as odd that an intelligent, educated and reflective woman should spend so much time and energy pursuing hazy promises, while never seriously asking what they promised. But I see that I was right to search as I did, although I misunderstood, insofar as I understood anything, what I might find. Not some lapidary truth expressed in a single revealing message, but what seems best described as 'understanding'. Which is not bestowed whole, in a moment of illumination. 'It takes a very long time', accumulating slowly, piece by piece, and never complete, though there is a 'take-off point' when one has enough understanding to feel one understands. Or at least is beginning to understand. The irrationality of grief is what allows (or needs) the illusion of a possible epiphany whose magnitude will balance the all-engulfing void of her death.

Believers of varied teachings would reject the interpretation of understanding as cumulative, referring instead to experiences of sudden illumination. I also have had moments of insight that seemed all-embracing and timeless, but they don't stay with me. I have not experienced conversion.

The Compassionate Friends Newsletter reports that some parents have been comforted by the suggestion that they should think of their child as having had a 'life complete', rather than 'a life cut short', since 'every life, no matter how long or short, is in truth a "life complete".'

At first sight it seems an odd consolation. Looked at one way it is a truism. A life that has ended is undoubtedly complete – nothing will be added to it. But at the same time it may also be a life cruelly robbed of years of living that it 'ought' to have had. Calling it 'complete' looks like finding consolation in a word. Describe something differently and it will appear different.

But then I reflect that this recommendation is basically the same as the advice I often give myself – to remember the life she had, and stop lamenting the life she didn't have. 'Complete' focusses attention on what was, and diverts it from what was snatched away. But why not say so more clearly? Because a word can hold mysterious power. We do often find consolation in a word.

I chanced on an article in *Le Monde diplomatique* by Tzvetan Todorov, in which he condemns the way some events in recent history, and especially the Holocaust, have become enveloped in an atmosphere of 'sacralisation' – there are things that cannot be said. Todorov insists that in the discussion of public affairs nothing should be sacred; only the truth should count. But, he adds, in the private life of each of us the sacred can have its place. 'If I have lost my child, I have absolutely no desire to see this event, for me absolutely unique, compared to other deaths, to other griefs.'

I feel a shock of recognition and gratitude. I have often thought something like this, even after experiencing the genuinely shared grief of a Compassionate Friends meeting. I know that tragedies as bitter as ours happen everywhere, and I do make comparisons with other deaths and other griefs, but I know also that for me her life and her death are unique and overwhelmingly significant – sacred. Todorov gives me the courage to assert that truth.

He leads me also in another direction, away from obsession with her death, to ask the meaning of 'sacred', and to consult dictionaries and encyclopaedias. Not an easy word to define. 'Set apart, to be approached with reverence, to be spoken of in some ways and not in others, arousing awe, wonder, admiration, astonishment and terror, numinous.' I learn that the classic discussions of 'the sacred' are by the French sociologist Emile Durkheim, and the German theologian Rudolf Otto, and half resolve to read them. But Durkheim is a forbidding writer, as I know from my days as a sociology student, and the London

Library has no copy of Otto's basic work. So I don't research further.

All this reading and questioning has added new words to my personal vocabulary. It has also given new meaning to familiar words, words I understood but would not myself have used, or not with the freight of meaning they have now. Such words include sacred. mystery, random, the void, closure, epiphany, spiritual, fulminating, chaos, cosmic indifference. And even simpler ones: bereavement, mourning, grief, acceptance.

I have often repeated Job's saying, 'The Lord gave and the Lord hath taken away,' but I didn't learn these words directly from The Book of Job. I knew its reputation as a canonic text, and felt I should read the whole poem, but although I had admired various anthologised extracts, I quailed before the task. It is long and, in the traditional Bible, looks forbiddingly dense; it has no easily perceived structure; the language is magnificent but cloyingly over-abundant. I abandoned several attempts to read it through.

All that changed when I got hold of a new translation and commentary. Several years ago, I read an enthusiastic review of such a book, by an American scholar, but I hadn't noted down the author's name and didn't know how (in pre-internet times) to trace it. Then by the sort of lucky chance that makes me fleetingly believe in a benevolent fate, I recognised an item in a catalogue of remaindered books, and sent for *The Book of Job, Translation, Introduction and Notes by Raymond P. Scheindlin, Professor of Medieval Hebrew Literature at The Jewish Theological Seminary of America.* Scheindlin's absorbing introduction places the text historically, analyses its structure, distinguishes the various speakers and discusses language and poetic form; the text is spaciously laid out and clearly articulated, and Scheindlin's translation reads easily and comprehensibly. Thanks to all these virtues, I have read and admired and enjoyed The Book of Job. Some of the verbal magnificence of the Authorised Version is lost, but this new translation is, nevertheless, splendid and moving. And I have both – Scheindlin's translation also works as an index to the Authorised Version. Without him I would never have come to know The Book of Job.

At first, his commentaries, although fascinating, seemed remote from my struggle to understand Sarah's death. His perspectives are wider and more general. I learned, for example, of the long-standing theological debate about the problem of evil and unmerited suffering, and added the term 'theodicy' ('a vindication of the justice of God in establishing a world in which evil exists') to my vocabulary. And Job's losses are so vast (sons and daughters, manservants and maidservants and sheep and cattle, and finally reputation, health and sleep), and his complaints are so self-centred, (no mourning for his untimely-sacrificed children) that I didn't feel any affinity between his mythical sufferings and Sarah's unique and deeply-resonating death. But some of Scheindlin's observations loop back to my experience. 'Job is never reconciled; his heart demands meaning, even though intellectually he intuits (and we know) that he cannot have it.' It is my situation essentially, and probably that of most non-believing contemporaries.

Scheindlin points out that one way in which the book works as consolation is by shifting attention from the injustice of suffering to the multi-facetted beauty of the world. He notes a contrast with Ecclesiastes, for whom life is wearying and pointless, while Job, despite his miseries, remains passionately in love with the world. As Sarah was. The moral for today seems to be, don't try to argue about injustice or guilt, don't expect anguish and longing to vanish, just allow yourself to be seduced by the gifts life still offers. Such as immersing yourself in The Book of Job for its own story and for the splendour of its poetry.

I have not returned to The Book of Ecclesiastes since I heard Douglas Gasking read from it at Sarah's funeral, but recent comments have prompted me to ask how I could have chosen to honour her death with a text so bleak. The obvious explanation is that it was the only relevant text that I knew. It said what I believed – that there is no survival after death; death is the end. There was also a certain defiance in the choice. I wanted no pious consolatory falsehoods. Only the purity of truth, however austere, was worthy of her.

But Ecclesiastes holds another message. Just as I covered her coffin with velvet and spring flowers, so the text I had chosen clothes its message in magnificent, mesmerising language. It is perhaps just that beauty of language that I rejected in subsequent broodings, wanting something plainer and tougher. But Ecclesiastes was the right choice then, and is still the right choice, infinitely preferable to the soothing falsity of 'Death is nothing at all.'

The taste for plain words has lead me recently to appropriate three new mottoes more stark than most of my earlier texts.

The first, from Victor Hugo, came suddenly to mind a few days ago, although I haven't looked at Hugo's poems on the death of his daughter for years. When I first read them, or rather those I found in anthologies, I thought them deplorably bathetic. Now I find myself repeating two lines whose flatness seems appropriate and satisfying:

Il faut que l'herbe pousse et que les enfants meurent;
Je le sais, o mon Dieu!
Grass must grow and children must die:
I know it, O God!

Next, Ted Hughes. Brooding over the myth of Orpheus after the death of Sylvia Plath, he imagined Pluto saying, 'No of course you can't have her back. She's dead, you idiot!' A salutary reproof, harsh, and wide-ranging. 'Of course she doesn't care about your loyalty. She's dead, you idiot!'

The third new motto is from Martin Amis's memoir *Experience*, in which he writes of talking to his father about the failure of an attempted reconciliation with his estranged wife, then living in the United States, and his sadness at being separated from his two sons. Kingsley commented:

> There's nothing you can do with things like that. You can only hope to coexist with them. They never go away. They're always with you. They're just – there.

In view of all this reading and searching and writing, I can hardly say that I found nothing to do, but at the end of it all, her death doesn't go away. It is always with me. It is just – there.

Hugo, Hughes and Amis imply that there is nothing more to be said. I can only carry the stone of her death in my heart and be glad for the scenes of past happiness that from time to time flash unexpectedly to mind.

I promised to send Ingrid, for the new baby, the blankets which I had bound with contrasting coloured ribbons for Sarah and Daniel when they were babies, so yesterday I fetched down from the attic the suitcase in which, long ago, I had packed away some of Sarah's belongings. I found it at the very back of the attic, streaked with black mould. So also, when I opened it, were some of the contents. There were two blue blankets, bound in pea green and deep pink. My lovingly-chosen colours remained vivid, but moths had eaten holes in the blankets; they were no fit present for a baby.

Under the blankets, huddled close together, some face down, were Sarah's stuffed animals – four koala bears, a kangaroo, a tiger and a penguin. They too had been attacked by moth. Kanga had no fur left; the bears had large raw patches and were covered in loose fluff and moth debris; Pinger, whose beak had already disintegrated through too much loving, had become even more dilapidated. The bears stretched out their stumpy arms towards me with expressions of entreaty and resignation, but in their lamentable state all I could do was to tumble the lot into a black plastic rubbish bag.

Their mute appealing faces stayed in my mind. I felt that I was betraying them, and Sarah who had loved them. It was late and I went to bed, but I didn't sleep, not wanting to lose the sense of tragic inevitability which brought me close, not to Sarah's lifetime but to the days immediately after she died, when I stared constantly at the overwhelming fact of her death and lulled myself at night with a strong sleeping tablet, but woke at four in the morning to confront the terrible knowledge again. She was still so near then that I could almost feel her physical presence.

I decided to rescue one of the animals, and this morning I brushed the soft loose fluff from the least-damaged bear. He didn't look too bad, after he had been steam-cleaned to destroy any remaining moth eggs. I dumped the other animals, with the blankets and the wrecked suitcase, in the community skip in Portobello Road, still feeling a mixture of betrayal and inevitability. The bears were dead, their bodies worthless, but their faces still spoke of dependence and hope. As Sarah's body, on the morning of the funeral, had been worthless, but the sense of her unique being was still powerfully present, demanding our care and protection.

I don't know what I will do with the rescued bear, but I remember that relics of the famous dead are revered by the most rational of unbelievers.

But that isn't all. Underneath the animals, wrapped in tissue paper, were several of Sarah's dresses, which I had kept when I gave away the rest of her clothes. The animals presented a scene of desolation, but the dresses are as bright and fresh as if she were about to choose one to wear. They speak of life, not of death. All day I have seen her firm sturdy body near me, wearing the orange cotton embroidered with white daisies, or the sleeveless blue gingham. The dresses bring back the atmosphere of happiness and security even more vividly than does a chance-discovered photograph. I am saving them for my granddaughter, Hannah.

Channel 4 has been showing a series of programmes entitled *Death*, which of course I started to watch. But I didn't continue – too external and too trite. It followed people dying of various terminal illnesses, describing their care and their relations with families, but saying nothing about what they think of their lives or their deaths. Well, almost nothing. Disappointed!

This week's TLS gives me words to define what I miss, in the review of a 560-page *Encyclopedia of Death and Dying*. It is published, by Routledge, at £85, so I shan't be buying it, and after reading the review by John Shand, I don't want to.

My main objection is perhaps directed at something the book does not attempt; it gives very little to mull over on the phenomenology of death and dying, and what our attitude ought to be towards it. Maybe the poets do this best, and oddly there is no entry for 'poetry' or indeed 'literature', although there is one for music.

There is a lot of information on matters related in all sorts of ways to death, but if one wants to reflect on death (as we often do, especially after someone we love has died), then one would be better off turning to the poets and writers, and indeed the philosophers ... The bent of the book, as often happens when studies are flagged as 'interdisciplinary' is, by a kind of default, mainly sociological (in the broadest sense to include history and psychology) and anthropological – a mantle of scientific disinterestedness. There is a considerable amount of material, but it is hard to see quite what holds it all together. There is very little scope in the book for reflection.

Well, my diary is about mulling over death and dying and what our attitude might be towards it, and perhaps I will be one of the writers to whom those who want to reflect on death turn (at least for hints as to where else to look). But often the content of such reflection is impossible to convey in words. The sudden immense change from life to death – one can *say* that it is immense, but that doesn't convey the awesomeness, the sense of profundity and hugeness, which one can contemplate and meditate on, silently and often, and still feel unable to comprehend or encompass it. That vague and disparaged word 'mull' is the right one. Read a poem or a perceptive memoir and mull over it.

I struggle to understand the chapter on Nietzsche and Rilke in Erich Heller's *The Disinherited Mind*. Most of it is too abstruse, but fragments almost reach me. He writes that their common aspiration is:
> to overcome the great spiritual depression, caused by the death of God, through new and ever greater powers of glory and praise, to adjust, indeed to revolutionise, thought and feeling in according with the reality of a world of absolute immanence, and to achieve this without any loss of spiritual grandeur.

A lofty and admirable aim! But how is it to be achieved? Heller continues:
> Rilke as well as Nietzsche discovers the fountainhead of joy in the very heart of the land of sorrow. Happiness for them is not, as it was for Schopenhauer, in the absence of pain; it is the fruit of so radical an acceptance of suffering that abundant delight springs from its very affirmation. Existence is pain and joy lies not in non-existence, as Schopenhauer would have it, but in its tragic transfiguration.

And that seems totally beyond me and perhaps beyond everyone, a drunken delusion. Certainly I come nowhere near it. And yet sometimes I get a glimmering of what it might be, when I remember Sarah's life without anguish. Once at least, Rilke helped me to attain that vision.

Ein Mal
jedes, nur ein Mal. Ein mal und nicht mehr. Und wir auch
ein Mal. Nie wieder. Aber dieses
ein Mal gewesen zu sein, wenn auch ein Mal:
irdisch gewesen zu sein, scheint nicht widerrufbar.
Once for each thing. Just once; no more. And we too,
Just once. And never again. But to have been
This once, completely, even if only once;
To have been at one with earth, seems beyond undoing.
[Translation Stephen Mitchell]

I read this, and feel a fierce exultation for her once-only life whose having-been can never be cancelled. Forgetting her death. As is right, because it is her life that existed for her. Only her life for her. It is for us that her death exists.

Rilke's poem gave me the experience of exultant acceptance, but it is not one I can return to easily. More often I summon up a calmer thankfulness for her presence on earth through Hardy's elegiac poems celebrating the indelible impress left on a landscape by an occasion of past happiness. But Hardy also speaks in a darker voice, as in 'Yell'ham Woods'. Eagerness, impetuous reaching out to the world, were attributes of her essential nature, which I feel blessed to have known – and that joyful optimism was slapped down by death. So 'Yell'ham Woods' also has a permanent place in my scriptures.

> Coome-Firtrees say that Life is a moan,
> And Clyffe-hill Clump says 'Yea!'
> But Yell'ham says a thing of its own :
> It's not 'Gray, gray
> Is Life alway!'
> That Yell'ham says,
> Nor that Life is for ends unknown.
>
> It says that Life would signify
> A thwarted purposing :
> That we come to live, and are called to die.
> Yes, that's the thing
> In fall, in spring,
> That Yell'ham says :-
> 'Life offers – to deny!'

'Life offers – to deny!' It seems a final incontestable truth. But not all the time. Hardy himself points out somewhere that because he expresses in a poem a particular attitude to life, it does not follow that he always thought or felt in that way. And reading such a poem both focusses awareness on a sombre reality, and offers compensating pleasures in its imagery, rhythm and compression.

Too much talk of death being a part of life. Death is the end and destruction of life, alien. To Sarah, to the countless victims of random violence, natural catastrophe or man-made disaster, to me soon of the depredations of age, to all of us death comes brutally from outside, for causes which have nothing to do with our character or beliefs or aspirations, or the dramatic shape of our lives, to stamp us out of existence.

When I think of my own impending death, the words that come most often to mind are those of Montaigne, in a saying whose idiosyncratic charm and relaxed syntax are untranslateable:

> Je veux qu'on agisse, et qu'on allonge les offices de la vie tant qu'on peut, et que la mort me trouve plantant mes choux, mais nonchalant d'elle, et encore plus de mon jardinage imparfait.
>
> I want us to be active, and to carry on the duties of life as long as we can, and may death find me planting my cabbages, not worried about it, much less about my unfinished gardening.

In other words – forget about death, get on with life! I like the homely metaphor of cabbage-planting. Montaigne doubtless never planted a cabbage in his life, and says elsewhere that he can't tell the difference between a cabbage and a lettuce. And somewhere else again he tells us not to worry about dying, since Nature will see to it for us.

I get a small sum every year, sometimes as much as £100, from the Authors' Licensing and Collecting Society for copying from *The Daniel Diary*, apparently for use in courses on child psychology or grief counselling. So someone still reads it. I am glad to know it, but that is not all I wanted for the book. I wanted 'the common reader' to enjoy it, and to admire and wonder at the courage, the clear-sightedness and the imaginative inventiveness that a very young child can achieve.

We think of the beloved dead every day of our lives, a commonplace of accounts of mourning, whose unanticipated truth I learned from experience. And yet with another person, even with a close friend, even with someone whom I know to have suffered a savage bereavement, I don't assume this constant awareness, and would not dare to refer to it unprompted.

Francisca Suñer grew up on the small island of Cabrera, near Majorca, a rural paradise over which her father presided as benevolent patriarch. When she was twelve, in the early days of the Spanish Civil War, her father and her two teenage brothers, guilty only of having rescued and succoured a pilot whose plane had crashed in the sea, were arrested by Nationalist troops, taken to Palma, and summarily shot. I knew that this tragedy had shadowed Francisca's life. We rarely spoke of it, or of Sarah's death, but the mutual experience of sudden outrageous death was part of our close friendship.

Shortly before her own death, Francisca related a conversation during which some opinion she expressed had prompted her husband to accuse her of forgetting the fate of her father and brothers. 'I told him that not a day passes that I don't think of them,' she said vehemently, with tears in her eyes. After 65 years. I was surprised, though I should not have been.

I have just washed and repaired the lining of my workbasket. 'A basket for holding clean clothes and toilet articles' was one of the necessities demanded by the nursing home where Sarah was to be born. 'You don't need a basket. A cardboard dress box will do,' a helpful nurse told me. But a cardboard box was not nearly good enough for me or my baby, and I bought a basket, not the flat open kind that, I subsequently learned, was intended, but a deep basket with handles. I lined it with white quilted nylon printed with little pink rosebuds, and made pockets for pins and ointments. It has been my sewing basket now for forty-five years, a part of Sarah's life that is still a part of mine. The spare satin buttons for her bright pink velveteen party-dress are in one of the pockets.

Also belonging to her life is the tan leather wallet which holds tickets and passport when I travel, and which I bought on the Champs Elysées, one sparkling September morning when she was sixteen months old. At £5, it was an extravagant purchase, but I wanted a purse slim enough to tuck into the basket on her pushchair. 'Pas de souliers!' exclaimed the girls who stopped to admire her as she sat in the sunshine, twirling her bare feet in vigorous circles. Years later, in the great romanesque abbey of St Séverin in Toulouse, the wallet was stolen by three little girls, who distracted my attention with a placard about their sick mother while they lifted it from my handbag. Eventually the wallet was returned, with my passport but no money or credit cards, by the British Consulate in Bordeaux. I cherish it now, like the sewing basket, as a token of continuity with the time of her time.

In my first enthusiasm for the essays in *Deuils*, I noted the titles of various books about death and mourning, and in Paris, on my way home that year, I managed to buy three of them, by Comte-Sponville, Julia Kristeva, and Vladimir Jankélévitch. I expected my appetite for reading about death and mourning to remain avid for the rest of my life, and regarded these books as a solid provision for the future. But when, soon afterwards, I put the Diary aside as finished (or so I thought), I was not attracted by such treatises. I dipped into each of them, but was soon defeated by their common qualities of immense length, slow-moving argument, copious repetition, reluctance to omit banalities, and close print. The three books sat on my shelves untouched.

Recently I looked again at *La Mort*, by Vladimir Jankélévitch. It has 466 pages, most of them without paragraph breaks, and presents all the above discouragements. I could not possibly read my way through it, and yet it gave me, again, the transforming shock of discovering a truth that, once stated, seems indubitable. In his introductory chapter, 'The Mystery of Death and the Phenomenon of Death', Jankélévitch distinguishes two utterly different aspects of death. On the one hand, it is a familiar empirical happening, an item in the daily news, an element in the everyday work of doctor and lawyer and bureaucrat and statistician, the expected end of all of us, a banality. And on the other hand it is an event unlike any other, a mystery, a 'meta-empirical happening', whose advent in our personal lives is always an astonishment, bringing consternation, disbelief, protest and bewilderment. Jankélévitch repeats his account of this contrast several times, in a rhetoric that is compelling and poetic. Death, he writes in one of his reprises, in its striking contrast to other events, has 'the symptoms of miracle'.

> [But], in contrast to supernatural apparitions, it is not a gain but a loss: death is a void which opens suddenly in the full onrush of being; an existence suddenly made invisible as if by some extraordinary conjuring trick, vanishing in the blink of an eye into the pit of non-being. And moreover this miracle is not a rare interruption of the natural order, an exceptional collapse in the course of existence, no, this miracle is at the same time the universal destiny of creatures...

Yes. Dr Jankélévitch, you are absolutely right, and I am grateful that you present this extraordinary double essence not as an emotional fantasy, but as something which just is, plainly there. Your discussion in 'The Mystery of Death and the Phenomenon of Death' belongs in my scriptures.

The citations from my personal scriptures that I have given

here, whether prose or poem, are only a fraction of the whole, and selected on no consistent principle. I am conscious that many books which were important to me in the early days are omitted because I read them before I started to keep my own Diary of Grief. Some poems that have reached me are omitted for a different reason – because they are well-known and frequently quoted. Repeated quotation in contexts of relatively low intensity tends to degrade great works, turning them into clichés, even if only temporarily. It is because they may be unfamiliar to English-speaking readers that so many of the poems included are in other languages.

But there is one astonishing and overwhelming English poem that I cannot ignore, though I will not quote it in full. Wordsworth's 'A slumber did my spirit seal' comes as near as words allow to being the majestic final statement of essential reality which I chased after for so long.

The bereaved want people to 'say something'. As Geneviève Jurgensen writes, 'There is absolutely no doubt that silence is open to the bleakest of interpretations. You have to come out of the woods into the open and say: I am here, I know, I have seen, I am witnessing, I am here. If you stay in the woods, you are saying just as clearly: I am not here. I know nothing. I have seen nothing. I am turning my back on you.' People, those others, know, too, that they should speak.

Pierre sent no words of sympathy when she died, but

I did not expect him to. He hadn't crossed to the other side of the street; he lived in Paris and sometimes years passed without our meeting. Forty years later, during a ceremonious lunch with Marie-Pierre and Erwin at the Brasserie Lipp, sitting next to me on the red leather banquette, Pierre said quietly, without preliminary, 'I didn't say anything when Sarah died because it was too sad.' He was ninety-two, suffering from emphysema (although he ordered veal shank, which he ate with relish), and we were not to see him again. He was fulfilling a duty before it was too late, and I felt touched and grateful.

Erwin and I both know that death looms near for us, though we agree that we should go on tending our cabbages without worrying about it. But, unexpectedly, Erwin told me that he would like his ashes to be scattered in the mountains, where we left Sarah's. Neither of us believes that it will matter in the slightest to him then – no him for it to matter to – and yet I take this wish seriously, solemnly even, and will carry it out should he die before me and I be still competent. It is a sign of the unstaunchable longing to be with her again.

Summary of Contents

I An Ending, 1964, pp 1-19
A farewell; the weekend; a day of illness; in hospital; the announcement; a first resolution; life continues; visiting the hospital; the Medical Director; arranging a funeral; viewing her body; Douglas Gasking reads Ecclesiastes; Nan Hutton's tribute; the need for funerals; pain and shock; struggling to understand; two reports; talking to Daniel and his reactions; looking for causes; the need to question; not weeping; letters of condolence; sudden silence; bereavement duties; talking about her; 'cooling the mark'; Cecily's visit; her positive response.

II First Questions, 1964-1965, pp 20-39
Strong beliefs? my non-belief; searching for alleviations, Blake; three personal arguments; singing to myself; finding other bereaved parents; Erwin's acceptance; turning to writing; a defence of writing about Sarah; reading; James Agee; John Gunther; Ernst Brücke; banality of tragedy; CaitlinThomas and Anne Philipe; Phyllis McGinley; Colette on a child's death; the Strudlbruggs; *The Poem Itself*; Paul Valéry; Bertold Brecht; Dostoyevsky.

III A Diary of Grief, 1965-1966, pp 40-51
Starting a Diary of Grief; Persistent expectation; Vaughn Springs and Bendigo; unique sorrow; girl on beach; luckier than some; cyclamen in the woods; an Australian picnic; madness; inner monologues; Circular Quay; Rushcutter's Bay; her lot; the ham actor; sorting possessions; continuing impossibilities; 'death stamped on her face' and a bureaucratic incident; Williamstown; good from evil; intensity of grief; IT IS; Lorne; Camo's moral.

IV Homecoming, 1966-1970, pp 52-77
Our stay in Melbourne; the return to London. Notes on the journey; returning home without her; taboos on places; a bereaved face; forgetting – mornings in bed; Daniel at school; Margaret; silent friends; Ommanney's cook; terror of memory; grotesque deaths; self images; selling pushchair; *The Story of Gabrielle;* summer evocation; Oliffe's story; living her death; why this book; more silent visits; her ashes; Shelley and Philipe; revisiting Henley; Joe Egg; relics; Freud to Binswanger; constantly thinking; madness and work; Aunt Julia and Grandmother Preston; Never glad confident morning; Goudeket on death of Colette; finding his destiny; 'nothing lost'?; fading anguish; losing closeness; no need to accept; Piero di Cosimo; 'never fully recovered'; no appropriate response; her mystery dries.

V New Ventures, 1970-1983, pp 78-115
Self-assessment; buying and developing a house; a place in Majorca; the City Lit. Pleasure of writing about her; not the worst; Como; discarding and keeping; Mrs Hockey; little

SUMMARY OF CONTENTS

that can be said; diaries of infancy – *Three Babies;* encouragement from Auden; Margaret's recognition; a City Lit piece; her spirit survives; Lehmann and Pike; self pity; continuing diaries? Mary Gilmore; reading lessons; Soller garage; Villequier and Hugo; Probate Office; Machado and Salinas; the Kalash; shoes; finish for her; art as murder; forgetful friends; Marsh Arabs; Siegfried Sassoon; *Tosa Diary;* Hardy and Hemingway; children in the garden; Helen Thomas's bewilderment; death as belittlement; '*Es mi Trini*'; Venice airport; Newson; Rush Rhees; Dr Adler's tactlessness; necessity and impossibility of talk; 'fulminating'; 'The Oxen'; other Hardy poems; memories of places; reliving happiness through writing; something done.

VI Something Done, 1983-1988, pp 116-132
First draft of SB; readers opinions; need for more work; finding Daniel Diary records; new solitude. Erwin's reaction; conversation with P; other readers' reactions; memorials and my aim; continuing unreality; Vanessa Bell on maternal instinct; André and happy memories; writing in second person; typing DD; return to atmosphere of first days; clinging to grief; lock of hair; three young girls remembered; Polyphemus and Shackleton; resting in the truth; Pamela Frankau; Christian McEwen; Queen Victoria; Lasch and acceptance; Mrs de Valera; Coe and the autobiography of infancy; lost sheep; her own fate.

VII Getting Published, 1988-1992, pp 133-174
Publishing The Daniel Diary; *rewards and disillusionments;*

remeeting with Alicja Iwanska. Radio Birmingham; Alicja's encouragement; Mary Shelley and Cynthia Asquith; François Jacob and non-belief; Kübler-Ross; all men are mortal; Allon White; end of mourning?; Festival of O-Bon; plane crash in Honduras; Henley's daughter; Rushdie on non-believers; Book Fair; formulae and Walter Ong; counting blessings; mourning what was; mourning the end of SB; SB written by a past self; Lionel Blue and playing your hand; dreams and plenitude; no interest in childhood as interpretation; reading about the Holocaust; Goethe's precepts; Ariès etc; exemplariness; writing about self or about them; Job, Schopenhauer and Comte-Sponville; Alicja and good fortune; Primo Levi on workmanship; grandeur of death; art and truth; Susan Lardner; Lesbia and twelvemonth; Danish therapy; Sciascia; Uhland; Rembrandt and Ardizzone; holiday in Sicily; more grotesque deaths, Montaigne; 'random'; strangers who lose by her death; bourgeois optimism; energy released by a death; Iris Origo; dark incomprehensibility; Dinnage's ramshackle structure and my scriptures; paid my debt.

VIII New Texts, 1993-1994, pp 175-202
Sending out SB again; comments of agents and publishers; a reply to criticism. Still living it; trying to serve reality; Bayley on Austen; taxonomies; reading elegies; Tittensor; the consolation of sharing; she dead and I alive; incomprehensibility; the appeal of established ritual; a defence of writing; ill-fitting words – Murdoch on Wittgenstein; Lewis and Barnes on recovery; vague phrases; Kochanowski; her serious gaze; shower thoughts; Wizard

of Oz; Heller and remembering beliefs; her death and mine; not music; a fulfilled life?; Christopher Ricks; *Flaubert's Parrot*; *Deuils*; Jean-Fred and phrases; Tours; complete acceptance?; International Gathering; Ramazani; Naipaul on pretending to write; Edith Evans; absolute renunciation? falling out of grief.

IX Afterwords, 2000. Infinity, pp203-238
Circulating a first draft of DG; an interval; resuming Diary of Grief entries without obsessional hope. Searching for what? contrary aims; burying in daily life; Mary Stott; Annie Dillard and why I write; Zagajeweski; Mounin's maxims; anthologies of death; humanist view; Hölderlin; *en pure perte*; Dan Taylor on authority; Henley's boast; Wieseltier, Edward Fitzgerald, Ecclesiastes; Berlin on God; memories of places, Tarn; personal change; understanding as the goal; a life complete; the sacred; new vocabulary; Scheindlin on Job; back to Ecclesiastes; plain words – Hugo, Hughes, Amis; Sarah's bears and dresses; encyclopedia of death; Nietzsche and Rilke; Yell'ham Woods; Montaigne on death; readers for The Daniel Diary; Francisca and remembering; workbasket and wallet; Jankélévitch; Wordsworth; Pierre; her ashes.

Acknowledgements

23   Lines from *Keep Right on to the End of the Road,* words and music by Harry Lauder and William A. Dillon. Reproduced by permission of Redwood Music Ltd and EMI Music Publishing Ltd.

36   Lines from 'Grosser Dankchoral', from *Selected Poems* by Bertold Brecht, published by Grove Press, NY, 1959. Reproduced by permission of Suhrkamp Verlag, Frankfurt.

60   Extract from *Fragrant Harbour* by F.D. Ommaney reproduced by kind permission of Frank Phillips.

93   Mary Gilmore: 'Nurse No Long Grief' and 'Nationality' reproduced with permission of NSW Trustee and Guardian, the Executor of Dame Mary Gilmore's Estate, and the publishers, ETT Imprint, Sydney.

139   Extract from *Too Close to the Bone* by Allon White, first published in *London Review of Books,* 1991. Reproduced by permission of *London Review of Books.*

142   Extract from interview with Ron Devereux published in the *Independent*, 20 October 1989. Reproduced by permission of the *Independent.*

157   Extract by Patrick Kavanagh from *A Book of*

ACKNOWLEDGMENTS

	Consolations (© Patrick Kavanagh 1992) is reproduced by permission of PFD (www.pfd.co.uk).
171	Extract from *Images & Shadows: Part of a Life* by Iris Origo. Reprinted by permission of David R. Godine, Publisher, Inc. Copyright © 1970 by Iris Origo.
228	Review by John Shand of *Encyclopedia of Death and Dying* first published in the *Times Literary Supplement*, 2001. Reproduced by permission of the *Times Literary Supplement*.
229	Extract from *The Disinherited Mind: Essays in Modern German Literature and Thought* by Erich Heller, published by Bowes & Bowes. Reprinted by permission of the Random House Group Ltd.

All reasonable effort has been made to trace the copyright holders of all extracts used in this work. Any copyright holder who has not been acknowledged is asked to contact Matador in order that the necessary permissions be requested and relevant alterations made.